I0198380

DEENDAYAL UPADHYAYA

Dr Shiv Shakti Nath Bakshi, a PhD in History from JNU, is currently the National Convenor of BJP Journals and Publication Department, and also Executive Editor of *Kamal Sandesh*.

He edits party publications, presents papers in India and abroad, writes regularly in many national dailies and is seen in panel discussions on various national TV channels.

DEENDAYAL UPADHYAYA
LIFE OF AN IDEOLOGUE POLITICIAN

Shiv Shakti Nath Bakshi

RUPA

Published by
Rupa Publications India Pvt. Ltd 2018
7/16, Ansari Road, Daryaganj
New Delhi 110002

Sales Centres:
Allahabad Bengaluru Chennai
Hyderabad Jaipur Kathmandu
Kolkata Mumbai

Copyright © Shiv Shakti Nath Bakshi 2018

The views and opinions expressed in this book are the author's own and the facts are as reported by him which have been verified to the extent possible, and the publishers are not in any way liable for the same.

All rights reserved.

No part of this publication may be reproduced, transmitted, or stored in a retrieval system, in any form or by any means, electronic, mechanical, photocopying, recording or otherwise, without the prior permission of the publisher.

ISBN: 978-81-291-xxxx-x

First impression 2018

10 9 8 7 6 5 4 3 2 1

The moral right of the author has been asserted.

Printed at Repro Knowledgecast Limited, India

This book is sold subject to the condition that it shall not, by way of trade or otherwise, be lent, resold, hired out, or otherwise circulated, without the publisher's prior consent, in any form of binding or cover other than that in which it is published.

In the loving memory of my parents,
Shyam Pyari Bakshi and Kartik Narayan Bakshi

CONTENT

PREFACE

Pandit Deendayal Upadhyaya, as an ideologue, organizer and political leader, left his indelible imprint on the canvas of Indian politics. As an organizer he laid the foundation of a political party which later emerged as an alternative to Indian National Congress; as an ideologue he imbued the political horizon with the originality of his ideas; and as a political leader he pursued the idea of principled politics in the country. He propounded the philosophy of 'Integral Humanism', and also tried to present an ideal picture of a political activist, the 'Karyakarta', through his conduct in public life. His intellectual capabilities, ideological commitment and political acumen still continue to inspire a large number of activists. His main contribution lies in building the edifice of Bharatiya Jana Sangh, nurturing its political culture, conceptualizing its political ideology and heralding the era of coalition governments in pursuance of creating an alternative to Congress and its politics.

Upadhyaya's life was full of challenges and difficulties. Both his parents died while he was still a child and his sibling left him at a very tender age. He also had to discontinue his studies due to adverse conditions at home. He came in contact with Rashtriya Swayamsevak Sangh (RSS) in 1937 in Kanpur while pursuing his graduation. It was a turning point in his life. He embraced the life of a 'pracharak' and became a full-time worker of RSS.

When Congress became a dominant force in national politics after Independence, many saw its policies and programmes as deviation from the ideals and ethos of the national movement and felt the need of an alternative political party. As a result, Bharatiya Jana Sangh was formed in 1951 with Dr Syama Prasad Mookerjee as its first President. After the mysterious death of Dr Syama Prasad Mookerjee, the responsibility to build the newly-born political party rested on the shoulders of Pandit Deendayal Upadhyaya, who initially became its General Secretary and later, its President. His ideas and actions have a deep imprint on the functioning, programmes, policies and organisational structure of Jana Sangh, and later Bharatiya Janata Party (BJP). Moreover, many activists and leaders who later became the leaders of BJP had a great deal of training under him. The ideological moorings of BJP are deeply entrenched in his philosophy of Integral Humanism. BJP has adopted the philosophy of Integral Humanism, as propounded by Pandit Deendayal Upadhyaya, as its core ideology. The party has now been focusing on Antyodaya, good governance, cultural nationalism, development and national security, while committing itself to the five basic principles called 'Panchanishthayen', all of which have their roots in Integral Humanism.

It has been attempted to decipher the journey from Bharatiya Jana Sangh to Bharatiya Janata Party and the impact of his ideas on the overall political culture and ideological and political evolution of the party. The book tries to analyze his political and ideological aspects and his contribution in the shaping of BJP. The governance and development models of BJP have been tried to be viewed in the contours of his ideals, writings and speeches. The book attempts to contextualize his vision, ideas, politics and the manner in which he sought to build Bharatiya Jana Sangh while seeking to create a niche for it in the non-Congress political space in India. It mainly discusses the historical circumstances in which the party was born and Pandit Deendayal Upadhyaya's role in making it a political force within a very short span of time. The book is written with an eye on the general readers who are eager to know more about him and the historical circumstances that led to the creation of Jana Sangh and its transition to BJP.

HIS JOURNEY

11 February 1968

30, Dr Rajendra Prasad Road, New Delhi—official residence of Atal Bihari Vajpayee

The silence was broken by the repeated ringing of the phone. As the sound grew shriller, Vajpayee's cook Birjoo rushed to receive the call. The news that was conveyed required to be passed on immediately. Vajpayee, then attending a meeting of Jana Sangh Parliamentary Party at 1, Ferozshah Road, received the news.

Pandit Deendayal Upadhyaya was found murdered.

It was a bombshell; unbelievable! The meeting was immediately adjourned.

The heart-rending incident was reported from Mughalsarai Railway Junction. At around 3.30 a.m. on 11 February 1968, a body was found lying by the railway track. It was discovered in the morning that the person found dead was Pt Deendayal Upadhyaya, the then President of Bharatiya Jana Sangh. The news spread in no time and a large number of Jana Sangh karyakartas started gathering in droves. Jana Sangh leaders and karyakartas across the nation were plunged into shock, grief and disbelief. Who could have committed this heinous crime? He was held in very high esteem as a leader of complete integrity, intellect and organizational ability, and known for his simplicity, humility and idealism. He was a man who knew no enemy, an Ajaatshatru in every sense of the word.

The murder of Pt Deendayal Upadhyaya still remains one of the unresolved mysteries of independent India.

ORPHANED CHILDHOOD

Nature processes destiny in its own ways. Many a time it creates obstacles in the path to greatness, tests a person though adversities and puts the exceptional challenges before the chosen ones. It fashions a person on the anvils of difficulties and moulds the persona only after it has faced the trials by fire. Pt Deendayal Upadhyaya was no exception.

On 25 December 1916, Deena, as Pt Deendayal Upadhyaya was nicknamed in his childhood, was born to Pt Bhagwati Prasad Upadhyaya and Smt Rampyari. His father was serving the Railways as station master of Jalesar Road Railway Station at the time of his birth. His mother was a deeply religious lady. Although 'Deena' was born in Dhanakia, Rajasthan, in the house of his maternal grandfather, his family originally belonged to Nagla Chandrabhan village in Mathura district, the birthplace of Bhagwan Krishna. Two years later, his brother Shivdayal was born.

Deena's early life was full of tragedies. When he was barely two and a half years old, the first tragedy befell his family; Pt Bhagwati Prasad Upadhyaya met an untimely death. The death of his father led his mother to go back to her father's home. His nana (maternal grandfather) was also a station master at Dhanakiya Road Railway Station. Deena and his brother Shivdayal could not get the love and affection of their mother for very long. Not even four years after their father's death, their mother left for her heavenly abode on 8 August 1924. Deena and Shivdayal were deprived of the love and care of their parents at a very young age. But tragedies were not to end with the death of their mother. Shortly after that, their nana also breathed his last. Now Deena and Shivdayal were under the care of their mama (maternal uncle). On 18 November 1934, Shivdayal also drew his last breath.

A BRILLIANT STUDENT

Deendayal stayed with his mama Shri Radharaman Shukla while pursuing his early education. His mama was in the Railways, posted at Gangapur, Rajasthan Railway Station. He received his education till the sixth grade in Gangapur, but had to stay at a residential school in Kota, Rajasthan, when he was in the seventh grade. He completed his eighth grade from Raigarh where his mama Shri Narayan Shukla was posted as a station master. He pursued his ninth and tenth grades from Kalyan High School, Sikar. He was a very sincere student and came First Class First in his tenth grade examination in 1935. His Geometry answer sheet was so good that the Rajasthan Board preserved it for many years. His brilliance was noticed by the royal family of Sikar, and Sikar Maharaj gave him an award of ₹250 and two gold medals. He was also granted a monthly scholarship of ₹10.

Deena's extraordinary talent was being noticed widely. His mama, Shri Radharaman Shukla, on seeing his performance at school level decided to send him to the prestigious Birla College, Pilani, for further studies. In Birla College he lived up to the expectations of his mama and stood first in the inter-college Board examination which earned him an award of ₹250, along with two gold medals, and a monthly scholarship of ₹10 from none other than Ghanshyamdas Birla. It was a great achievement for Deendayal.

Deendayal shifted to Kanpur in 1937 for further studies. He joined Sanatan Dharma College and took up Mathematics, Sanskrit and Hindi, apart from English, as his subjects in BA Programme. Even there he topped the merit list and was granted a scholarship of ₹30 per month.

He then joined St. John's College, Agra in 1939 to pursue MA in English literature. He secured first position in the MA Previous exam, but had to leave his studies due to adverse conditions back home. His cousin Rama Devi was seriously ill, and being deeply attached to her, he preferred to attend to her during her illness. But despite his best efforts, he could not save her. It gave him a severe jolt and he could not appear for his MA final exam. His education was discontinued. On the insistence of his mama, he appeared for the administrative examination, and qualified. However, with his eyes set on larger goals, he was more eager to serve the nation. He went to Allahabad to pursue a Basic Training (BT) course.

EARLY DAYS IN RSS

Rashtriya Swayamsevak Sangh (RSS) was founded in 1925 and its work was spreading to different parts of the country. RSS was attracting young students and teachers who were joining the organization for a nationalist cause. Deendayal was initiated into RSS through one of his close friends, Balwant Mahashinde. He had come to Kanpur with Balwant and stayed at a hostel. He joined the RSS shakha of the hostel under the influence of Balwant. In 1937 he formally took the oath and started hoisting the Sangh flag in the shakha. He became the gatnayak of the hostel gat.

As a swayamsevak in Kanpur, he participated in 40-day Officers Training Camps (OTC) of the Sangh in 1939 and 1942. These camps used to be held only in Nagpur in those times. After spending time at these camps, he was more convinced and dedicated to the nationalist cause. He was determined and strong-willed. While everyone was impressed with his intellectual abilities, he concerned himself with analyzing the problems that the Indian society faced, and was convinced of the need of disciplined and dedicated swayamsevaks in the society. Completely convinced of the ideas and methods of RSS, he decided to dedicate his life to serve the nation through the Sangh work. While it was a decision which had far-reaching implications on his personal life, the nation was to see the emergence of a thinker and karmayogi who would lay the foundation of future politics in the country.

Deendayal decided to become a lifelong pracharak in 1942. It was a very tough decision. A pracharak is supposed to live a life like a sanyasi, without marrying, and work fulltime to serve the nation by strengthening the Sangh work. In a letter to his mama on 21 July 1942, he expressed his deep desire to work as a pracharak of RSS, 'Can we not forgo a few worthless ambitions for the benefit and protection of the society and for the faith for which Rama suffered exile, Krishna bore innumerable hardships, Rana Pratap roamed about forest to forest, Shivaji staked his all and Guru Gobind Singh allowed his little sons to be buried alive?'[1]

He started his work as a pracharak from a Tehsil in Lakhimpur district of Uttar Pradesh. His commitment to the cause, ability to mix with everyone, humility, intellectual capacity and dedication helped him win the hearts of people. From the rich and educated to the poor, destitute and deprived sections of the society, everyone was fascinated by his personality and started drawing closer to Sangh activities. His tireless efforts and organizational abilities helped him to win the support of both the rural and urban masses.

His organizational abilities and talent did not escape the notice of his seniors in Sangh. He was given the responsibility of Sah-prantpracharak of Uttar Pradesh in 1945. At that time, Shri Bhaurao Deoras was the prant-pracharak of Sangh in Uttar Pradesh. Deendayal's responsibilities started increasing with every passing day, and he proved himself efficient on a number of occasions, taking initiatives and implementing them with success.

Deendayal had a testing time when Sangh was banned in 1948

---

[1]Sharma, Mahesh Chandra, *Deendayal Upadhyaya: Sampoorna Vangmaya*, vol. I, Prabhat Prakashan, 2016, p. 4.

by the Congress government. RSS decided to launch satyagraha in response to the ban. Deendayal organized the satyagraha, employing his effective organizational capabilities and strategic acumen. The Congress, which had become weary of the growing popularity of RSS and took the extreme step of ordering the ban on Sangh, found itself stunned to see the discipline and dedication of RSS satyagrahis who never resorted to violence even in the face of extreme provocation by the police. The attempt to crush the satyagraha with an iron hand resulted in strengthening of voices in support of the RSS. Thousands of swayamsevaks participated in the satyagraha, and while police resorted to violent suppression of the movement, the satyagrahis remained committed to the principles of non-violence. Not a single incident of violence by the satyagrahis was reported. Deendayal, who was organizing and planning the satyagraha, never lost his cool. Appreciating the qualities of Deendayal, Guruji Golwalkar had said that he was adept in the art of keeping the mind cool while having a burning fire in the heart. The fire in his heart could never reach up to his mind to disturb his mental balance, and neither could the coolness of his mind come down to extinguish the fire that his heart had. This quality was in full display during the satyagraha when Deendayal maintained his composure and allowed the movement to keep its momentum.

He not only kept the movement on the ground alive, but also found out a way to keep the ideological struggle active and uninterrupted. As a result of the ban on RSS, the magazine set up by Deendayal, *Rashtradharma*, was also banned. But Deendayal's pen could not be reined in; he immediately started another publication, *Panchjanya*. *Himalaya* came out the same day *Panchjanya* was banned. As soon as *Himalaya* was attacked, *Desh Bhakta* was started. In this way, he maintained the continuity of the ideological struggle through his relentless efforts and skills.

Bhaurao Deoras wrote about the tireless efforts, dedication and organizational skills of Deendayal in strengthening RSS work in Uttar Pradesh: 'In the early days of your Sangh work, when your path was strewn with thorns, you set out on this difficult task. No one was familiar with the Sangh activities in Uttar Pradesh at that time. You took over the onerous responsibility on your shoulders as an ordinary swayamsevak. You really laid the foundation of the Sangh work in Uttar Pradesh. Today, the RSS work in the province is a result of your hard work and sense of duty. Many of our volunteers have been inspired by the examples set by you. You have been a constant source of inspiration to all of them. You are an ideal swayamsevak. We had heard of the ideal swayamsevak from our founder, you embody all these qualities in yourself. A brilliant intellect, an unequalled sense of duty, modesty and humility—you symbolize all of them in your person.'[2]

Another remarkable contribution of Deendayal was the development of a think-tank in RSS, called Education Cell. It was formed by Bhaurao Deoras, Deendayal Upadhyaya and Nanaji Deshmukh.

WRITER AND THINKER

Apart from his organizational capabilities, skills and dedication, Deendayal was a writer par excellence. He was an original thinker and philosopher. He believed in intellectual awakening of the nation, and for this he wielded strong writing on almost every issue. He wrote two literary pieces—*Samrat Chandragupta* and *Jagadguru Shri Shankaracharya* in 1946 and 1947 respectively. *Bharatiya Artha Niti: Vikas Ki Ek Disha* (Indian Economic Policy: A Direction of Development) is a brilliant work that captured his economic thinking. 'Rashtra Chintan' and 'Rashtra Jivanki Disha'

---

[2]Gupta, Tansukhram, Pt. *Deendayal Upadhyaya Ka Mahaprayan*, Surya Bharati Prakashan, New Delhi, 2008, p. 68–69

are collections of his articles written on the issues related to nation, society, politics, dharma and culture.

He wrote *Samrat Chandragupta* in a single night. In 1946, Bhaurao Deoras, the then prant-pracharak of Uttar Pradesh, lamented in a meeting that inspirational literature for children was not available in simple and lucid language. Deendayal, who was listening to him quietly in the meeting, worked throughout the night so that he could show his work to Bhaurao Deoras in the morning. The preface of the book was all the more interesting as he wrote, 'The readers of this book need not be told everything about the maze of historical facts. It would suffice them to know that the events in this book are true despite the concerted efforts of European scholars and their blind followers among the Indian historians to distort them and to serve their own purpose and vested interests'. In *Jagadguru Shankaracharya*, he tried to present glorious intellectual traditions of the past in contemporary situations of a changed world which was demanding similar rigour and intellectual vitality. In an interesting exposition about the 'sanyasa', which explains the very basis of the life of a sanghpracharak, he described the concept as enunciated by Shankaracharya himself, 'This sanyaas does not mean being aloof from people; it means adopting them. It does not mean renunciation but compassion. Yes, this compassion does not lead to attachment or tie us down; it is not narrow or confined, it is vast; it is not weakness but our strength. Sanyaas does not mean abdicating one's social responsibilities; it means fulfilling them with vigour, selflessly.'

In *Bharatiya Artha Niti: Vikas Ki Ek Disha*, he pointed out the main malady in policy making. He wrote that the direction for the future was not based on thinking about the present with an understanding of the past, which resulted in different theories by historians, economists and politicians. He called for a coordinated effort which he tried to present by emphasizing on economic ideas, including those in Indian traditions; fundamental priorities; demand

and industrial priorities; small and big industries; trade; transport; and social service.

Rashtra Chintan is a collection of his nineteen important speeches that highlight the ideological positions on crucial issues. These speeches are: 1. Rashtrajivan Ki Samasyayen (Problems of National Life), 2. Bharatiya Rajniti Ki Ek Maulik Bhul (A Fundamental Mistake of Indian politics), 3. Samvidhan Ka Kya Karen? (What Should be Done with the Constitution?), 4. Rashtrabhasha Ki Samasya (Problem of National Language), 5. Akhand Bharat, Sadhya Aur Sadhan (Undivided India, Means and End), 6. Rashtriyata Ka Punya Pravah (Holy Flow of Nationalism), 7. Swatantrata Ki Sadhna Evam Siddhi (Struggle and Attainment of Independence), 8. Lokmat Ka Niyamak Kaun Ho? (Who Should be the Regulator of People's Will?), 9. Samajwad, Loktantra Aur Hindutvavad (Socialism, Democracy and Hindutvavad), 10. Loktantra Ka Bharatiyakaran (Indianization of Democracy), 11. Vikendrit Artha-Vyavastha (Decentralized Economy), 12. Shiksha (Education), 13. Sahi Shabda, Sahi Artha (Right Word, Right Meaning), 14. Chiti (Soul of the Nation), 15. Untitled, 16. Untitled, 17. Rashtratma Va Vishwatma (National Soul and World Soul), 18. Dharmarajya Kya Aur Kyon? (Dharmarajya: What and Why?) and 19. Dharma Dharna Se Hai (That Which Sustains is Dharma).

Rashtra Jivan Ki Disha is a collection of eighteen speeches and writings. It includes: 1. Param Sukh Ka Marg (Path to Greatest Happiness), 2.'Main' aur 'Hum' ('I' and 'We'), 3. Rashtra ki Jeevandayini Shakti (Life Giving Power of the Nation), 4. Rashtra aur Rajya (Nation and State), 5. Rashtra Ka Swarup–Chiti (Form of Nation–Chiti), 6. Secular: Arth-Anartha (Secular: Meaning Distorted), 7. Rashtra: Prakriti Aur Vikarti (Nation: Nature and Distortion), 8. Lokmat-Parishkar (Purifying People's Will), 9. 'Param Vaibhav' Nayatu Metatswarashtram (Highest Glory), 10. Sangathan Ka Aadhaar: Rashtravad (Basis of Organization:

Nationalism), 11. Vyakti Aur Samaj Ka Sambandh (Relation Between Individual and Society), 12. Samanjasyapurna Samaj Vyavstha (Balanced Social System), 13. Doun Raah Na Payi (Not Getting Both Paths), 14. Vikendrikaran (Decentralization), 15. Guru Puja: Swadeshi-Videshi (Teacher worship: Indian and Foreign), 16. Hamara Rashtradhwaj (Our National Flag), 17. Vijay Akanksha (Desire of Victory), 18. Saransh (Jivan Darshan) (Synopsis (Philosophy of Life).

Deendayal wrote the book *The Two Plans: Premises, Performance and Prospects* on five year planning, in English, which was discussed in the economic circles. Apart from these he also wrote booklets, among which *Hamara Kashmir* (Our Kashmir), *Mahan Vishwasghat* (Great Treachery), *Akhand Bharat* (Undivided India), *Tax ya Loot* (Tax or Loot) are famous.

He used to write almost regularly in *Panchjanya* and *Organiser*. In *Organiser* he used to write a column called 'Political Diary'. He believed in expressing himself on the issue of the day and engaged in debates, explaining the ideological position which was crucial in guiding the activist working even at ground level. He was also involved in the publication of many organizational magazines. He was one of the inspirations behind the publication of weekly *Panchjanya* and monthly *Rashtradharma*, which were started in 1945. Later, *Swadesh* was started with Deendayal as its editor.

JANA SANGH

Jana Sangh was founded by Dr Syama Prasad Mookerjee as an alternative to Congress politics, which was seen to be deviating from nationalistic concerns under Nehru. Dr Syama Prasad Mookerjee had the support of RSS as a result of the then Sarsanghchalak Guruji Golwalkar's agreement with Dr Mookerjee on nationalism. In one of his articles, Guruji Golwalkar wrote, 'When an agreement was reached I chose my tried and tested associates who were selfless and strong willed and those who could shoulder the burden of a new party...It was in this manner that Dr Mookerjee could realize his ideal of founding the Bharatiya Jana Sangh.'[3] One of the leading names among the pracharaks who were sent to Jana Sangh by Sangh to help Dr Syama Prasad Mookerjee build a new political party, was Pt Deendayal Upadhyaya.

On 21 September 1951, when the first state conference of the Uttar Pradesh Jana Sangh was held in Lucknow, resolution to give the party a national form was piloted by Deendayal and, as a result, just within one month, on 21 October 1951, a national conference was held in Delhi and Dr Syama Prasad Mookerjee became its first president.

In December 1952 a huge national conference was held in Kanpur. In this conference, out of the 16 resolutions passed, eight were written and proposed by Pt Deendayal Upadhyaya. The resolutions prepared by him give an insight into his grasp over a wide range of issues and ideological depth. The resolutions were: 1. South Africa's Apartheid Policy, 2. Foreign Pockets, 3. Pit-falls in the First Plan, 4. Rehabilitation of the Displaced Persons, 5. Amend the Election Law, 6. Massive Constructive Programme, 7. Cultural Revival and 8. Agitation Against Sales Tax.

The rest of the resolutions were: 9. Exodus from East Bengal, 10. Swadeshi Movement, 11. Jana Sangh Constitution, 12. Integrate Kashmir Movement, 13. Urdu Agitation, 14. States Reorganization, 15. Merger of Hyderabad and 16. Full Support to RSS Demand for Ban on Cow Slaughter.

In this session, Dr Syama Prasad Mookerjee declared Pt Deendayal Upadhyaya as National General Secretary of Jana Sangh. This decision was in accordance with the basic concept of the organization wherein collective leadership was the guiding

---

[3]Sharma, Mahesh Chandra, *Pandit Deendayal Upadhyaya*, Publication Division, Ministry of Information & Broadcasting, Government of India, New Delhi, 2004, p. 30

principle. It was a well-considered decision which proved to be a momentous one for the party. Bala Saheb Deoras later explained that Upadhyaya was chosen by Guruji Golwalkar because he could formulate political philosophy of Jana Sangh as per Indian philosophy, and despite being in politics he could remain detached from power politics, and finally, because he could build a team dedicated to the cause of the uplift of the country. Dr Syama Prasad Mookerjee was so impressed by the organizing capacity, skill and intellect of Pt Deendayal Upadhyaya, that he once said, 'If I could get two more Deendayals, I will change the whole political map of India'[4]

Pt Deendayal Upadhyaya shouldered this responsibility for fifteen years till he became the president of Jana Sangh in 1967.

During the Kashmir Satyagraha when Jana Sangh raised the issue of *'Ekdesh me ek pradhan, ek vidhan aur ek nishan'* (One head, one law and one symbol in the country), Deendayal was given the responsibility to steer the movement across the country. Dr Syama Prasad Mookerjee was himself participating in the Satyagraha. He said he got, in Deendayal, a friend as he wished.

Soon the news of Dr Syama Prasad Mookerjee's martyrdom arrived. It was a big jolt for a political party which had just started to make its mark. The responsibility to take the party forward fell on the strong shoulders of Deendayal. While Premnath Dogra, Maulichandra Sharma, Bachhraj Vyas, Pitamber Das, Dr Raghuvir, A. Ramarao and Balraj Madhok became party presidents at different times after the martyrdom of Dr Syama Prasad Mookerjee, Deendayal continued to expand the party organization as all India general secretary till 1967. He was able to create a unique identity of Jana Sangh through his relentless organizational activities and intellectual leadership.

---

[4]Raje, Sudhakar, (Ed.), *Pt. Deendayal Upadhyaya: A Profile,* Deendayal Research Institute, New Delhi, 1992, p. 13.

Deendayal contested elections only once in his lifetime. It was a by-election held in 1963 after the Chinese aggression. Nehru's leadership was facing stringent criticism in the wake of Chinese aggression, and his China policy was under attack. People were also facing wartime emergency and other hardships. The by-elections were announced for four places. It was because of the great efforts of Dr Ram Manohar Lohia that the Opposition fielded joint candidates against the Congress. Dr Lohia himself contested from Farrukhabad, Acharya Kriplani from Amroha, Swatantra Party General Secretary Minoo Masani from Rajkot and Pt Deendayal Upadhyaya from Jaunpur. While all the other three candidates won, Deendayal lost the election. Deendayal was not in favour of contesting the election, and neither did his mentor and guide Guruji Gowalkar wanted him to, but Bhaurao Deoras wanted him to take a plunge in electoral politics. Golwalkar had said before the election that whether he wins or loses, it will be a loss either way. Although he was a joint candidate of the Opposition, he was still opposed. Dr Lohia himself strongly condemned this treacherous act publicly.

This by-election brought forth a different dimension of his political thought which was based on practising the principles which he preached. He did not allow himself to be swayed away by the temptation of victory and was not afraid of defeat. Jaunpur, from where he was contesting, was seen as a stronghold of Rajputs and Brahmins. Congress was trying to woo the Rajput voter which could have been countered by raising Brahmin sentiments. When the local people insisted Deendayal to use his Brahmin caste to gain votes, he not only resisted but strongly said, 'If you resort to such means, I shall withdraw my candidature.'[5] He said that an election could be won by resorting to such means, but Jana Sangh would lose the election. Although Deendayal lost the election, a

---

[5]Ibid, p. 36.

positive environment was created for Jana Sangh. Deendayal was able to build a unique image of Jana Sangh.

Pt Deendayal Upadhyaya was elected president of Jana Sangh in the 14th annual session held on December 29–31, 1967 in Calicut. His presidential address in the session is still a historic record which gives an insight into the ideological and political mission of Jana Sangh. He adorned this post for only forty-three days as he was found murdered in the early morning of 11 February 1968 in Mughalsarai.

HIS MURDER

Come, let us consider every drop of Panditji's blood as the holy mark on our foreheads and move forward the ideals he lived and worked for. We should take every spark from his funeral pyre to our hearts and work with our utmost dedication like he did. We should turn the bones of this Dadhichi into stones and hurl them on the enemies so that our sacred soil is free of all roadblocks.

A small lamp has been extinguished. We will have to fight darkness by lighting our lives, the Sun has set, we will have to find our ways in the light of the stars. Our friend, our companion, our guide has gone. We will have to cherish his sacred memory and move on to achieve our objectives.[6]

These lines are quoted from the article 'We accept the challenge' written by Atal Bihari Vajpayee on the murder of Pt Deendayal Upadhyaya. He further said:

Party's session was held in Calicut. We went there. The session was a grand success under his presidentship. The people said the Jana Sangh had presented a great display of commitment

---

[6]Ibid, pp. 162–163.

and ideology. People had concentrated all their hopes and aspirations under Panditji. People from India and abroad said that Jana Sangh had acquired a new identity at the Calicut session. In reality, there was a change in the perception of people rather than a change in Jana Sangh. Some among these people were those in whose eyes reflected the sin within their hearts, a spark of jealousy and sense of violence. They could not digest this change of scene, and today they have deprived us of Pt Deendayalji. No one is sure about the circumstances in which he died. A person for whom millions of people were ready to sacrifice their lives and were bound together under him, was pushed into the lap of death in the dark night far away from his followers and countrymen.[7]

L.K. Advani recounted his feelings:

When he came back from Calicut session, I said to him, 'Deendayalji, we will provide you a steno; he will be with you all the while and write everything for you, even in the train. You should not travel all alone. There should at least be one person with you throughout. We will arrange everything.' Even when he was leaving for Mughalsarai from Delhi, we went to meet him and repeated our request but he replied, 'No, thanks. I can look after myself and I'll do the writing, too, all by myself.' My only regret remains that had Deendayalji paid heed to my suggestion, history would have been different. But destiny had wished otherwise. Who could change it?[8]

As the budget session was about to start, a meeting of the Jana Sangh Parliamentary Party was scheduled in New Delhi and a meeting of the Bihar Jana Sangh State Executive was slated to

---

[7]Jha, Prabhat (Ed.), *The Ajaatshatru Deendayalji*, Dr. Mookerjee Smruti Nyas, New Delhi, 2011, p. 06.
[8]Ibid, pp. 08–09.

take place in Patna. Deendayal was supposed to be present in the Jana Sangh Parliamentary Party meeting in New Delhi, but he also got an invitation from Bihar and preferred to be present in the Patna meeting. He requested Sunder Singh Bhandari, the General Secretary of the Party, to be present in the New Delhi meeting. He was travelling from Lucknow to Patna by Pathankot-Sialdah Express to attend the Bihar meeting. This was the fateful journey in which he was murdered and his dead body was found in mysterious circumstances in Mughalsarai.

The news of Deendayal's murder evoked a huge sense of loss and resentment. A feeling of helplessness engulfed everyone in Jana Sangh and a sense of shock, combined with mystery, compounded the feelings of grief and pain. It was unspeakable and the circumstances were wrapped in the layers of doubts and disbeliefs. A body was found lying on the railway track near electric pole no. 1276 in Mughalsarai. It was spotted by a leverman at around 3.45 a.m. on 11 February 1968, who quickly informed the assistant station master. The body was brought to the station and declared 'dead' by the doctor. Till that time no one even imagined that the dead person was Jana Sangh President Pt Deendayal Upadhyaya. It was only when his body was brought to the railway station and a curious crowd gathered that a railway staff identified it. The news spread wide and fast in no time. The nation was plunged in grief. The Jana Sangh karyakartas started gathering on the railway station in large numbers. The news was conveyed to Delhi.

On hearing the news of Deendayal's murder, Guruji Golwalkar rushed to Varanasi, where Deendayal's body was brought. He touched Deendayal's face with his hands and brought them to his eyes in reverence. He said:

> Many people run their family and hence they can imagine what this is like. I do not run a family, hence my grief is a thousandfold. Hence I will not say anything about him. Just

that, Deendayal was taken from me by God. I had read an old English saying somewhere, 'Whom the gods love, die young.'[9]

Shri Guruji in his condolence speech said, 'The mind is overcast with grief. The skein of this tragic event will be unraveled by those whose business is to do so. Whatever their enquiries bring to light, the Sangh has lost in Deendayal Upadhyaya dedicated worker who had started fulfilling the promise of his youth. Now we are deprived of the rich harvest of his versatile genius.'[10]

Balasaheb Deoras, General Secretary of Rashtriya Swayamsevak Sangh, while remembering Deendayal, recalled, 'Shri Upadhyaya was my close friend and younger brother. This unexpected event has left me stunned. I remember my friendship with him for the last 30 years, and I do not know how I can convince myself that he is no more. He was a versatile individual and successful worker. He entered politics with a pure life and his effort to purify politics is the most important aspect of his life.'[11]

President of Bharatiya Jana Sangh, Atal Bihari Vajpayee, said:

Shri Upadhyaya was not a member of Parliament, but if the credit of the victory of all the Jana Sangh members, present here as well as in the other House, and of building up the Jana Sangh should be given to only one individual, then that individual is Shri Upadhyaya. His simple living, fundamental thinking, organizational skill, long-range vision, and the quality of taking everybody around him along with him on the path of progress—all these will prove guiding lights for the coming generations. Inspite of being highly educated he

---

[9]Sharma, Mahesh Chandra, *Pandit Deendayal Upadhyaya*, Publication Division, Ministry of Information & Broadcasting, Government of India, New Delhi, 2004, p. 159.
[10]Raje, Sudhakar, *Pandit Deendayal: A Profile*, Deendayal Research Institute, New Delhi, 1992, p. 43.
[11]Ibid, pp. 34.

did not take up a job, nor did he get himself tied down to family life. He dedicated every ounce of his energy and every moment of his life to the noble task of working for the happiness of Bharat Mata.[12]

Senior Jana Sangh leader Prem Nath Dogra said, 'It is not possible even to imagine the circumstances in which Shri Deendayal's body was found. It is all a mystery. Shri Upadhyaya's death has not only been a personal loss for me but a serious loss for the unity and integrity of the country.'[13]

While the entire country was in shock, tributes started pouring in from all eminent luminaries of the day, across political spectrum.

President Zakir Husain, in his message said, 'I was deeply shocked to learn of the death of Shri Deendayal Upadhyaya. I express deep sympathies for the members of the family of the departed leader.'[14]

Vice-President V.V. Giri said, 'Shri Upadhyaya was a great son of Mother India. His death is a matter of great grief. In his passing away, India has lost a great nationalist and dedicated person.'[15]

Prime Minister Indira Gandhi, in her message said, 'I have been greatly shocked at the news of Shri Upadhyaya's death. Shri Upadhyaya was playing a leading role in the political life of the country. His untimely and unexpected death in such tragic circumstances has left his work incomplete. Whatever the differences between the Jana Sangh and the Congress, Shri Upadhyaya was the most respected leader and he had dedicated his life to the integrity and culture of the country.'[16]

---

[12]Ibid, pp. 32–33.
[13]Ibid, pp. 33–34.
[14]Ibid, p. 29.
[15]Ibid
[16]Ibid, pp. 29–30.

Lok Sabha Speaker Neelam Sanjiva Reddy said, 'Shri Upadhyaya was a selfless and dedicated worker. The country will be poorer by his loss.'[17] Charan Singh, the Chief Minister of Uttar Pradesh in his message said, 'Shri Upadhyaya was a leading figure in the public life of the country. The news of his death was a great shock. Public life in this country has suffered a great loss in his death.'[18] Finance Minister Morarji Desai said, 'Shri Upadhyaya was a dedicated patriot and a politician of high character. He had great reverence for Indian culture and dharma, and great faith in the unity and integrity of the country. Because of these qualities in him I had great respect for him, even though I did not know him personally. Shri Upadhyaya had been completely dedicated to his ideals, and it is on the strength of such dedicated patriots that the nation rises high in the world. His death is sudden and mysterious. The Central Government will give full cooperation to the State Government in its enquiry into his death.'[19]

Union Minister in the Ministry of Communications and Parliamentary Affairs, I.K. Gujral said, 'The late Pt Deendayal Upadhyaya was one of the foremost leaders of independent India. He had great humility and simplicity in his behaviour. He also had extraordinary organizational and leadership qualities. He was respected as a sobre and liberal leader.'[20]

Senior Statesman C. Rajagopalachari said, 'Shri Upadhyaya was one of the great thinkers in our political field.'[21] According to Sarvodaya Leader Jayaprakash Narayan, 'In the death of Shri Upadhyaya the country has lost an able and the Jana Sangh its greatest leader.'[22] Well-known author K.M. Munshi said, 'With the

---

[17] Ibid, p. 30.
[18] Ibid
[19] Ibid, p. 31.
[20] Ibid, p. 32.
[21] Ibid, p. 34.
[22] Ibid, p. 35.

death of Shri Upadhyaya India has lost a great son. The country has lost a great champion of integrity and democracy.'[23]

COVERAGE BY MEDIA

The unfortunate incident was widely reported in media. All the newspapers were unanimous in condemning the incident and called for an investigation into the gruesome murder of Deendayal. The editorials and press reports also gave an insight into the life, contribution and political significance of Deendayal for the nation. *Hindustan Times*, published from New Delhi, commented on its editorial page, 'The death of Mr Deendayal Upadhyaya, President of the Bharatiya Jana Sangh, assumed particularly tragic proportions because of the moderating role he was playing in his party. This is a moment of trial for the Jana Sangh. Whoever is elected (President in his place) can do no better than emulate the example of Mr Upadhyaya, who in private life as in public displayed the supreme quality of leadership—of securing the support of the maximum number of people on any issue of importance.'[24]

The Statesman, published from New Delhi, wrote, 'Mr Deendayal Upadhyaya's death at the age of 51 would have been tragic in any case, but the circumstances in which it has occurred during a railway journey make it doubly sorrowful. The suspicion that he has been the victim of murder rather than an accident has been voiced by several leaders of the Jana Sangh and strengthened by some of the circumstantial evidence. It is imperative therefore that the enquiry into the tragedy, which the U.P. Government has already ordered and to which Mrs Gandhi has promised all possible help from the Centre, is conducted with the utmost thoroughness and maximum possible speed. Death has not only brought to a premature end a

---

[23]Ibid, p. 35.

[24]Sharma, Mahesh Chandra, *Deendayal Upadhyaya: Sampoorna Vangmaya*, vol. XV, Prabhat Prakashan, 2016, p. 199, *Hindustan Times*, 13 February 1968.

promising political career but has created a void in the Jana Sangh's leadership.'[25]

The Indian Express, published from New Delhi, said, 'The sudden death of Deendayal Upadhyaya is a grievous loss to the nation. A soft-spoken and gentle person, he built an impressive structure on the political foundation laid by Syama Prasad Mookerjee. In a relatively brief period he enlarged a small group into a formidable national party. It was characteristic of the man that he shunned the limelight and chose to work quietly as General Secretary of his party. It was only a few months ago that he became the President of his party, but he had been its real leader for more than a decade. His gentle exterior concealed stern conviction and remarkable strength of character. His dedication to what he regarded as the country's true national interest was absolute. Whatever one might think of his political conviction and ideology, even his opponents were compelled to recognise the basic honesty of the man. But for his untimely death at the relatively young age of 51, he would surely have enhanced his national stature in the years to come. The circumstances of his death must cause general concern.'[26]

The Tribune from Chandigarh read, 'The sudden death of Mr Deendayal Upadhyaya is a loss not only for the Bharatiya Jana Sangh but also for the entire country. That Mr Upadhyaya should have held the office of General Secretary for 14 successive years is a measure of the degree with which he had identified himself with the party and of the confidence which his leadership inspired in the rank and file. Mr Upadhyaya, barely 50, had just entered the most fruitful period of his life and hence the deep and widespread grief in the country by his sudden death in tragic circumstances.'[27]

The Hindi newspaper, *Hindustan*, published from New Delhi,

---

[25]*The Statesman*, 13 February 1968.
[26]*The Indian Express*, 13 February 1968, republished in *Organiser*, 18 February 1968.
[27]*The Tribune*, 13 February 1968.

commented, 'The mystery of Shri Upadhyaya's death still remains a mystery. There should be a full inquiry into his death. But the country will long for another Deendayal and this desire would not be easily fulfilled. He was not only the President of the All-India Jana Sangh but was a dedicated leader for the country, with great promise. He was born of that soil which is required for the healthy growth of democracy.'[28]

Another national Hindi daily *Navbharat Times*, New Delhi, commented, 'Shri Upadhyaya was one of those few leaders who are known for selfless and unostentatious service of the people. His life was like the lamp that lights the path for others. While time fills up all deficiencies, the loss caused by his death has come at a time when both the Party and the country needed him very much.'[29]

HIS LAST JOURNEY

As the shocking news reached Delhi, Atal Bihari Vajpayee, Balraj Madhok and Jagdish Prasad Mathur rushed to Varanasi on a special aircraft arranged with the help of the government. It was decided to perform the last rites in Delhi. The body was brought to Varanasi after postmortem, where a large number of Jana Sangh leaders had gathered. RSS Sarsanghchalak Guruji Golwalkar, Prant-pracharak of UP Prof. Rajendra Singh, Deputy Chief Minister of UP Ram Prakash Gupta, along with a large number of Jana Sangh leaders and karyakartas, gathered the airport to bid adieu to their karmayogi. The aircraft took off from Varanasi airport with Deendayal's body, accompanied by Atal Bihari Vajpayee, Balraj Madhok and other leaders, to Delhi.

In Delhi a large number of leaders and karyakartas had gathered at Palam Airport. As the aircraft landed at 11.30 p.m. in Delhi, the

---

[28]Raje, Sudhakar, (Ed.), *Pt. Deendayal Upadhyaya: A profile*, Deendayal Research Institute, New Delhi, 1992, p. 41; Hindustan, 13 February 1968.
[29]Ibid

atmosphere became heavy at the sudden turn of events. Deendayal had become the hope of millions of party karyakartas and the news of his murder instilled a sense of loss and anguish, and left a lingering pain in their hearts. L.K. Advani and Vijay Kumar Malhotra went inside the plane to pay their respects. As his body was brought out of the plane, the air was rented with the sound of 'Long live Deendayal'. The spectacle of grief-stricken people jostling for his sight, with tears in their eyes was extremely tragic. Amid the showering of flower petals, the body was taken to the ambulance kept ready to take it to the official residence of Atal Bihari Vajpayee.

The body was kept at 30, Rajendra Marg for the last darshan. A simple and sensitive karmayogi, relentless activist, thinker and organizer par excellence, friend, philosopher and guide to countless karyakartas, true swayamsevak and ideal leader was lying calmly, integrated to that supreme being in whom everyone should find solace in submergence. Amid the chanting of the shlokas of Shrimad Bhagwad Gita, people were coming to pay their last respects from all corners of the country. Everyone was mourning and the entire Delhi was plunged in grief. The shopkeepers had put their shutters down and offices were closed. People were proceeding to 30, Rajendra Prasad Road. The crowd continued to swell and the police and RSS Swayamsevaks had a difficult task in managing it. People were emotionally moved on seeing his body while paying their respects by showering petals and offering garlands. Eyes were filled with tears struggling to remain confined, but overflowing intermittently. This tragedy had left everyone shocked. Who could have killed him, an Ajaatshatru who knew no enemy? There was no answer to it and it was making the situation more intolerable and unbearably painful. President Zakir Husain came to offer his tribute in the morning. Prime Minister Indira Gandhi and Deputy Prime Minister Morarji Desai also offered their tributes. Jayaprakash Narayan, along with his wife, visited the place to offer his tributes in the afternoon. Chief Minister of Uttar Pradesh Chaudhary Charan Singh and Chief Minister of Punjab Laxman Singh Gill also paid their tributes. Leaders, social workers, cultural personalities from different sections of the society came to pay their last respects. A large number of people gathered at the venue to pay their respects to the departed soul.

Amid chanting of mantras and slogans of 'Long Live Deendayal', the funeral procession began at around 1.00 p.m., and his body was placed in the specially decorated saffron ratha with Jana Sangh flags on it. The gathering of leaders and karyakartas became emotional observing the final journey of their leader. They started showering flower petals and garlands while chanting *Ram Nam Satya Hai'*. The entire street was lined up with karyakartas and leaders who were walking in front of the ratha. More than a hundred bikes and many bicycles were also part of the funeral procession. The Chief Executive Councillor of Delhi's Metropolitan Council, Vijay Kumar Malhotra, and many ministers from different states were seen walking in the procession. The mayor of Delhi, Lala Hansraj Gupta; cousin of Deendayal, Prabhu Dayal Shukla; former Pracharak Vasantrao Oak and Sundersingh Bhandari were on the ratha. Jagdish Prasad Mathur was seated beside the driver's seat. The procession moved slowly by the closed shops of Janpath, and people lined up on the sides of the streets, showering flower petals on the ratha. At around 02.00 p.m., when the procession stopped for a while, various market associations in Janpath paid their last respects. From Janpath the procession entered the famous Connaught Place market, the centre of attraction in Delhi, which was calmly waiting for the ratha to arrive. The Chief Minister of Jammu & Kashmir, Bakshi Ghulam Muhammad, paid his tributes there and then the procession moved through Odean road, Minto Road Bridge and Thomson road which were filled with crowds on both sides. From top of houses, people showered flower petals and garlands on the ratha as a mark of respect.

The procession then proceeded to Ajmeri Gate where a small programme was held on the specially constructed dais adorned by his picture. Representatives of various market associations, along with senior Jana Sangh leaders, offered their tributes. While Atal Bihari Vajpayee and Balraj Madhok now sat on the ratha, Sarkaryavah Balasaheb Deoras, Bachhraj Vyas, Pitambar Das, Nanaji Deshmukh and Sundersingh Bhandari accompanied the procession. Deputy Chief Minister of UP, Ram Prakash Gupta and Deputy Chief Minister of Madhya Pradesh, Virendra Kumar Sakhlecha also walked in front of the ratha, leading the procession. The procession entered Chawri Bazar after crossing Nai Sadak, and reached Chandni Chowk, the historic market of Delhi. In Chandni Chowk, elaborate tributes were offered at three places. Firstly, Delhi Mercantile Association offered its tribute in the form of a huge garland that was hung across the road and descended on the ratha when it reached there. The second was at the historical fountain near Gurudwara Shishganj where special announcements were made from the Gurudwara over mic, and white clothes and flowers were offered. The third tribute was paid by Arya Samaj Diwan hall where Aryadhwaj (flag of Arya Samaj), garlands and flowers were offered to the body. The procession then started for its final destination, the Nigambodh ghat. People lined up on both sides of the road gave a tearful farewell amid the chanting of mantras and slogans, and showering of flowers and garlands.

Nigambodh ghat located on the bank of river Yamuna is the main cremation ground in Delhi. The procession had reached its final destination at around six in the evening. The body was taken on a platform amid the chanting of sacred mantras. The body was placed on the pyre and final rites began. At 6.45 p.m., the program of last tribute began. RSS Sarkaryavah Balasaheb Deoras was the first to offer his tributes. He was followed by Lala Hansraj Gupta, Sanghchalak of Nagpur Balasaheb Ghatate and Madhavrao Mule. Thereafter, L.K. Advani, Vijay Kumar Malhotra,

Pitambardas, Yagyanarayan, Balraj Madhok, Atal Bihari Vajpayee, Jagannath Rao Joshi, J.B. Kriplani, Ram Prakash Gupta, Virendra Kumar Sakhlecha and others paid their tributes. The final moment had come. Sandalwood was placed over the body and holy water was sprinkled on the pyre. At 7.06 p.m., his maternal cousin, Shri Prabhudayal Shukla ignited the funeral pyre. At 7.23 p.m., the Kapalkriya happened and the mortal remains of Deendayal Upadhyaya merged with the five elements.

HIS MURDER, STILL A MYSTERY

The murder of Deendayal, the then National President of Jana Sangh, sent a shockwave in the entire nation. The mysterious circumstances in which his body was found made the situation more complicated as no clue, whatsoever, was found to relate to the actual cause of the murder. Although the investigations were handed over to CBI and Chandrachud Commission was instituted, his murderers could not be found. As questions were raised over the sincerity of the government of the day, Nanaji Deshmukh wrote, 'It was not Jana Sangh alone but even the Session Judge of Varanasi who disbelieved the CBI story that two petty thieves had murdered Panditji. Our counsel made it very clear to the Enquiry Commission that we did not have any proof. We only placed before the Commission what information came our way. It was the business of the Commission to go onto these bits of information and further investigate the matter and unravel the mystery. This the Chandrachud Commission failed to do.'[30] J.P. Mathur, while expressing similar doubts, wrote, 'Deendayalji's untimely death is shrouded in mystery, even today. It is hard to digest that he was killed by some unknown thieves. I can recall how the course of the inquiry into his death changed. His dead body was found on

---

[30]Ibid.

the railway track covered with a chaddar. It never looked like a case of ordinary murder.'[31]

It was for the third time that Jana Sangh was jolted by the untimely demise of its leader—first it was Dr Syama Prasad Mookerjee's death under doubtful circumstances during his confinement in Kashmir in the course of Kashmir movement, second it was Dr Raghuvir, a man of eminence, who succeeded him met his untimely death and third when Deendayal was murdered mysteriously. These were testing times for the young party and its leaders had to struggle hard to carry forward the baton and to maintain its continuity without any break. Guruji Golwalkar rightly said in Deendayal's funeral oration that there was a tradition of workers who came forward after one another, and hence 'No place will remain vacant, no post unmanned.' The Jana Sangh, after Deendayal, continued to be guided by his work and ideas, and the BJP, even today, feels inspired by his work and makes efforts to tread on the path shown by him. Deendayal is no more as a mortal being, but his ideas and contributions remain inscribed in the pages of independent India.

---

[31]Ibid, p. 21.

THE MAKING OF
BHARATIYA JANA SANGH

If one person has to be given credit for building and expanding Jana Sangh, then he is Upadhyayaji. He was a man with simple tastes. Yet he was an original thinker, adept organizer and visionary leader, whose quality of taking everyone ahead will always serve as a guiding force for the new generation. He did not join government services even after pursuing higher education, he did not tie himself with the bondage of family, he offered every part of his body and every second of his life for decorating the head of Bharat Mata with the vermilion of fortune.[32]

—Atal Bihari Vajpayee

Indian National Congress was in the forefront of Indian freedom struggle under the leadership of Mahatma Gandhi. As a political party it launched nationwide movements under Gandhi's leadership, articulating national sentiments against the

---

[32]Atal Bihari Vajpayee's tribute to Deendayal Upadhyaya in the Lok Sabha on 12 February 1968, Sharma, Chadrika Prasad (Ed), *Kuchh Lekh, Kuchh Bhashan*, Kitabghar Prakashan, 2012, p. 236.

colonial rule and mobilizing people through agitations as well as constructive programmes. The colonial rule had to negotiate with the Congress which was the representative of Indian people at various stages. This gave Congress a pre-eminence among all the other political parties and voices in the country, and when the time came for the transfer of power, the power was transferred to the government headed by Pt Jawaharlal Nehru in 1947. It was followed by the formation of the Constituent Assembly and drafting of the Indian Constitution in which Congress played a dominant role. Congress was seen as an umbrella organization having the capacity to adjust and accommodate different voices within the country and unite them in national interest. The only problem with the Congress politics was that it could not stop the partition of the country on communal lines, yet people had reposed their complete faith in the Congress even in the post-partition India. Congress was still seen representing the largest sections of the Indian society which was trying to come to terms with a divided India.

In post-independence India, Congress became the only political party having a national presence with an organizational network. There was practically no challenge to the Congress's claim of having inherited the legacy of freedom struggle, and it was seen as a natural ruling party which could replace the colonial rule. It had become a dominant force in the country. It tried to take along all the voices in the country with the initiative to include almost everyone in the Constituent Assembly after the formation of Pakistan. Leaders like Baba Saheb Bhimrao Ambedkar and Dr Syama Prasad Mookerjee were given representation in the Cabinet and a message was sent across to the people that Congress was seeking to lead a united India. In the initial days of democracy, the foundation needed to be strong. It could only be achieved by uniting the prominent voices who could lend support to the process of building an India on the basis of unity and integrity. At this crucial juncture India stood united, dreaming to translate its liberation from the clutches of an alien rule into the concept of swaraj and swatantrata. It cannot be denied that the foundation of the Indian Constitution was laid on the glorious national movement, which saw the people's urge for independence transforming India into a democratic republic, united and looking forward to a new future.

As India was becoming secure and confident as a nation, Indian politics, too, started maturing and looking for avenues for alternative experiments. The murder of Mahatma Gandhi on 30 January 1948 and demise of Sardar Vallabhbhai Patel on 15 December 1950 created a huge vacuum in the Congress. Pt Jawaharlal Nehru remained the only towering figure in the Congress whose writ started running unchallenged in the party. Under him, Congress policy and programmes were seen as a drift from the ideals and ethos of national movement, and many saw Congress falling in the grip of Nehruism. In such a situation, the necessity of a new political party was started to be felt by many leaders and political activists. There was a feeling to explore an alternative course of action which could politically challenge the hegemonic presence of Congress. The resignations of Dr Syama Prasad Mookerjee and Dr B.R. Ambedkar may be seen in this context as attempts to create alternatives to Nehru's politics and Congress policies in the post-independence era.

RESIGNATION OF DR SYAMA PRASAD MOOKERJEE

Dr Syama Prasad Mookerjee was recognized as a renowned political figure, Hindu Mahasabha leader, educationist and intellectual of highest order. Born on 6 July 1901 in a very highly respected family in Calcutta (now Kolkata) to father Ashutosh Mookerjee, a High Court judge and Vice Chancellor of Calcutta University, and mother Jogmaya Devi, he entered Bengal legislative assembly as Calcutta University representative in 1929 as a Congress candidate, but resigned next year when Congress boycotted the legislature, only to return as an independent candidate later. He was the Opposition leader in the state assembly when Krishak Praja Party Muslim League coalition was in power during 1937–41. Later, he became the Finance Minister, during 1941–42, when he joined Progressive Coalition government headed by Fazlul Haque, but he soon resigned. He gradually emerged as a voice of Hindus and joined Hindu Mahasabha in 1944 and also became its president. He advocated tolerance and communal harmony and opposed partition initially, but the Noakhali massacres, in which Hindus were mercilessly killed in large numbers, changed his views and he felt that Hindus were no longer safe under the rule of Muslim League government in united Bengal. He led a campaign to rescue Hindu majority areas from falling under the dominance of East Pakistan. He was later invited by Nehru to join his Cabinet as Industry and Supply minister.

Mookerjee and Nehru fell out on the signing of what is known as Nehru-Liaqat Pact of 1950. The pact was signed by the prime ministers of India and Pakistan on 8 April 1950 in New Delhi, whereby both countries were to make provisions for their minorities. The pact was seen as a big compromise by Dr Syama Prasad Mookerjee who felt that India cannot abdicate its responsibilities vis-à-vis the minorities in East Pakistan who were facing continuous persecution by the Pakistani authorities. In his 'Foreword' to the book *East Bengal Minorities since Delhi Pact*, he wrote:

> The problem is essentially political and raises questions affecting basic human rights. Normally speaking, Pakistan being a separate territory, no foreign country can have any obligation regarding the treatment of Pakistani citizens by their own government. We cannot, however, forget the circumstances under which India was partitioned in 1947 and the assurances that were held out to the minorities by those who are in

authority today regarding their future rights and privileges. No section of non-Muslims wanted partition of India and those non-Muslims who had to live in Pakistan after partition did so mainly on account of such pledges given by the leaders of Indian public opinion specially belonging to Congress. Since Pakistan has failed to fulfil her obligation in this behalf, India has to face her responsibility and protect the minorities.

The condition of minorities was miserable in Pakistan. Pakistan was formed on the basis of two-nation theory of Muslim League and it had declared itself to be an Islamic state. The minorities were at the mercy of the Pakistani authorities which were highly communalized, sectarian and intolerant. In such circumstances, relying on the assurances of Pakistan was considered a big mistake. On the other hand it was considered a responsibility of India to ensure safety, security and citizenship rights to the minorities in Pakistan, given the circumstances in which India was partitioned. Dr Syama Prasad Mookerjee, in a statement in the Parliament on 19 April 1950, said:

> When the partition of this country became inevitable I played a very large part in creating public opinion in favour of the partition of Bengal, for I felt that if it was not done, the whole Bengal and also perhaps Assam would fall to Pakistan. At that time little knowing that I would join the first Central Cabinet, along with others, I gave assurances to the Hindus of East Bengal stating that if they suffered at the hands of the future Pakistan government, if they were denied elementary rights of citizenship, if their lives or honours were jeopardized and attacked, Free India would not remain an idle spectator and their just cause would be boldly taken up by the Government and people of India.[33]

---

[33]Mathur, J.P., *History of Bharatiya Jana Sangh*, Bharatiya Janata Party, vol. 6, 2006, p.88.

The cabinet meeting in which Nehru-Liaqat Pact was discussed could not arrive at a consensus. Dr Syama Prasad Mookerjee resigned immediately after returning from the Cabinet meeting on 6 April 1950. In the letter addressed to Nehru while resigning from the Cabinet he wrote:

> The agreement which, I suppose, will be finalized today does not touch the basic problem and is not likely to offer any solution. I can under no circumstances be a party to it. Apart from the fact that it will bring little solace to the sufferers, it has certain features which are bound to give rise to fresh communal and political problems in India, the consequences of which we cannot foresee today. In my humble opinion the policy you are following will fail. Time alone can prove this.[34]

On resigning from the Cabinet Dr Syama Prasad Mookerjee got a rousing reception in Delhi and West Bengal. A grand reception was organized in Delhi on 19 April 1950 in which RSS Sanghchalak Lal Hansraj Gupta, Pracharak Vasantrao Krishna Oak, Lala Yodhraj and Pt Maulichandra Sharma were present. The reception was presided over by a leading businessman of Delhi, Shri Prakash Dutta Bhargava. There were expectations that Dr Syama Prasad Mookerjee would give leadership to the country. *Organiser* published details of the reception, outlining a feeling which was part of the address to Dr Syama Prasad Mookerjee, in which it was said:

> One who shows the way in such critical occasion is a leader. The country needs such courageous leadership and we the citizens of Delhi are confident that you will now give such lead to the country as it will not be based on lack of hope and abject appeasement of the enemy.[35]

---

[34]Letter from Dr Syama Prasad Mookerjee to Jawaharlal Nehru on 6 April 1950, communicating his resignation.

[35]Mathur, J.P., *History of Bharatiya Jana Sangh*, Bharatiya Janata Party, vol. 6, 2006. p. 88–89.

He was a very popular figure in West Bengal and his resignation filled the people with a new hope and enthusiasm. In a public reception organized for him on 21 May 1950, more than three lakhs of people turned up. He was seen as a bold and true leader who was ready to raise the issues in the interest of the people. The *Organiser* reported the reception in which the address to him was concluded in following terms:

> The masses stunned, desperate and agitated, are waiting for a powerful lead, a lead that will not know of any compromise with injustice, which if necessary, will, in the cause of justice, even unfurl the banner of revolt. Bengal is eagerly waiting for such a lead.[36]

FORMATION OF JANA SANGH

Soon after the country became independent and the nation was partitioned, a new kind of political situation prevailed in India. After the murder of Gandhi, Rashtriya Swayamsevak Sangh was banned and a political conspiracy was being hatched in the country to suit certain ulterior political motives. After the death of Sardar Patel, Nehru started to display his dictatorial tendencies more resolutely. In the absence of both Gandhi and Nehru, the Congress slipped into the grip of Nehruism. Issues like minority appeasement, license-permit-quota raj, neglect of national security, surrender on the national issues like Kashmir, and compromising stand affecting India's interest on international forum started stirring the conscience of the nationalist people of the country. Dr Syama Prasad Mookerjee, deeply hurt by India's silence on the persecution of minority Hindus in East Pakistan and perturbed by the policies pursued by the Congress government under the

---

[36]Ibid, p. 89.

influence of Nehruism, resigned from the Nehru Cabinet. At the same time, some RSS swayamsevaks started to realize that their 'principled-distance' from politics had resulted in their getting politically alienated and targeted by those with vested interests to score political points. In such a situation, the necessity of a nationalist political party began to be felt by the nationalist and democratic-minded people of the nation. In Sangh, a debate started on the merit of forming a political party.

Rashtriya Swayamsevak Sangh as an organization had declared itself above politics and dedicated to cultural regeneration of the nation. But the ban on RSS in the wake of Mahatma Gandhi's murder made many swayamsevaks to rethink their position in politics. While a vilification campaign was unleashed against Sangh, no one came forward to defend it. Nevertheless, it was exonerated from the charges. At the same time, there was some kind of pressure for the Sangh to join Congress. Sarsanghchalak Guruji Golwalkar had, in an interview to *Organiser* on 25 October 1948, said:

> After the ban has been lifted and swayamsevaks have an opportunity to meet together, they can if they like, convert the Sangh into a political body. That is the democratic way. I for myself cannot say anything. I am not a dictator. Personally, I am outside politics... Why people should drag us into politics? We are happy with them as politicians and ourselves as swayamsevaks.[37]

In a letter written to Sardar Patel, Guruji Golwalkar had replied to his call to join Congress in the following terms:

> At the outset let me make it clear that the RSS is not a political party with any ambition for political power in the country. All these years of its existence it has steered clear

---

[37]Ibid, p. 71.

of politics with its party rivalry and scramble for power…
It leaves all its members free to choose and to subscribe to
whatever political outlook they prefer and to join and work
in the party of their choice.[38]

The malicious campaign against the Sangh had left a deep feeling
of alienation, and a sense of hurt was prevailing among the
swayamsevaks. A debate was raging within Sangh whether to
join politics or not. The sentiments of those pleading for a new
political party could be understood from the manner in which it
was expressed by K.R. Malkani in a series of articles published in
the *Organiser*:

> Sangh must take part in politics not only to protect itself
> against the greedy designs of politicians but to stop the un-
> Bharatiya and anti-Bharatiya politics of the Government and
> to advance and expedite the cause of Bharatiyata through
> state machinery side-by-side with official effort in the same
> direction. Sangh must continue as it is, an 'ashram' for the
> national cultural education of the entire citizenry, but it must
> develop a political wing for the more effective and early
> achievements of its ideals.[39]

The resignation of Dr Syama Prasad Mookerjee created an
opportunity wherein the voices supporting the formation of a new
political party grew stronger. As already said that prominent Sangh
swayamsevaks were present in the reception given to Dr Syama
Prasad Mookerjee in Delhi, swayamsevaks like Vasant Rao Oak and
Balraj Madhok kept in touch with Dr Mookerjee and they started
thinking about forming a new political party. Guruji Golwalkar
recounted this in 1956 in the *Organiser*:

---

[38]Ibid, p. 71–72.
[39]Ibid, p. 72.

One of my old colleagues who had developed a liking for political work to a degree uncommon and undesirable for a swayamsevak of the RSS, Shri Vasant Rao Oak, was in close contact with him for a long time as his association seems to have prompted Dr Mookerjee to seek my cooperation and help in the matter... Naturally I had to warn him that the RSS could not be drawn into politics, that it cannot play second fiddle to any political or other party since no organization devoted to wholesale regeneration of the real, i.e., cultural life of the Nation could ever function successfully if it was tried to be used as a handmaid of political parties.[40]

Dr Syama Prasad Mookerjee had earlier desired Sangh to be converted into a political party, but that was not to happen. Dr Mookerjee met Guruji Golwalkar several times between 1949 and 1950 to discuss the formation of a political party, and finally Guruji Gowalkar allowed 'its (RSS) workers to cooperate and collaborate with Dr Mookerjee for the formation of a party which might reflect their view points on national questions.'[41] In one of his articles Guruji Golwalkar wrote, 'When an agreement was reached, I chose my tried and tested associates who were selfless and strong-willed and those who could shoulder the burden of a new party... It was in this manner that Dr Mookerjee could realize his ideal of founding Bharatiya Jana Sangh.'[42] He further wrote, 'Both of us (Dr Mookerjee and Guruji Golwalkar) did not make any move without consulting each other in respect of our organization and work areas. While doing this, we also took care that we did not interfere in each other's domain or that there was no conflict between the objectives of the two organizations. Nor should one be seen as

---

[40]Ibid, p. 90.
[41]Sharma, Mahesh Chandra, *Pandit Deendyal Upadhyaya*, Publication Division, 2004, p. 30.
[42]Ibid.

overtaking the other.'[43]

As a result, on 5 May 1951, Dr Syama Prasad Mookerjee announced the formation of People's Party in Calcutta which was followed by the formation of Bharatiya Jana Sangh at state level. The first unit was the Punjab unit, consisting of what are now Punjab, Haryana and Himachal Pradesh, formed on 27 May 1951 in Jalandhar. The unit was formed under the presidentship of Balraj Bhalla and included Mauli Chandra Sharma as vice-president and Balraj Madhok as secretary. The Delhi unit was formed under the presidentship of Vaidya Guru Dutta. The state units were formed in UP, Rajasthan, Madhya Pradesh, Karnataka, Gujarat, Bihar and Assam within the next three months. On 2 September 1951, Uttar Pradesh unit was formed with Rao Krishna Pal Singh as president and Pt Deendayal Upadhyaya as secretary. On the same day a meeting was held in Indore and Madhya Bharat unit was formed where Badrilal Dave was elected president and Manoharrao Moghe was elected secretary. The Rajasthan-Ajmer unit was formed with Chiranjilal Sharma as president and Sunder Singh Bhandari as secretary on 13 October 1951. Thereafter, state-level units were formed in Karnataka, Vindhyas, Bihar, Assam, Gujarat and Surashtra. An all-India convention of Jana Sangh was called in which some like-minded regional parties, like Praja Parishad in Jammu and Swadheen Jana Sangh in Orissa were also invited. Bharatiya Jana Sangh was formed on 21 October 1951 in Raghomal Girls High School, Delhi, with Dr Syama Prasad Mookerjee as its first president. The convention was attended by about 500 delegates where it was resolved to merge all the state/provincial units into a national party in the name of Bharatiya Jana Sangh.

---

[43]Ibid.

IDEOLOGY OF JANA SANGH

In his Presidential Address, Dr Syama Prasad Mookerjee stated:

> We have thrown open our party to all citizens of Bharat
> irrespective of caste, creed, or community. While we recognize
> that in the matter of customs, habits, religion and language,
> Bharat presents a unique diversity, the people must be united
> by a bond of fellowship and understanding inspired by deep
> devotion and loyalty to the spirit of a common motherland.
> Our party will strive to work for that unity in diversity which
> has been the key-note of Bharat's culture and civilization.[44]

The party had firm faith in the underlying unity of India; it
recognized the diversity as its strength and unique feature. It was
widely felt that contrary to the expectations of the people, the
Congress under Nehru was moving towards continuing the same
colonial approach vis-à-vis education, culture, governance and even
economy. It was seen as going back from the commitment which
the leaders of the national movement had made to the people. It
was also felt that Congress under Nehru was trying to impose alien
ideas and ideologies, and was reluctant in taking inspirations from
India's roots and was blindly following foreign patterns in almost
all fields. Jana Sangh was formed in response to the prevailing
situation where an alternative was sought to be built as a historic
necessity. In its constitution, the objective of the Jana Sangh has
been expressed in following terms:

> The aim of the Bharatiya Jana Sangh is to make India a
> political, social and economic democracy on the basis of
> Bharatiya sanskriti and maryada. In this democracy every
> individual shall have equal opportunity and freedom.
> This democracy shall be oriented towards making India a

---

[44]Ibid, p. 94.

prosperous, powerful, organized, progressive, modern and alert nation, which may successfully contain the aggressive tendency of other countries and play an effective role in the international sphere in establishing world peace.[45]

The first manifesto released in 1951 by the party assesses the then prevailing situation in following terms:

> The mistaken policies and 'abharatiya' and unrealistic approach to the national problems by the Party in power is primarily responsible for this state of affairs in the country. In their anxiety to make Bharat carbon-copy of the West, they have ignored and neglected the best in Bharatiya life and ideals. They have failed to harness the enthusiasm created by freedom to the task of realization of the great potentialities of the country.[46]

The Manifesto also talked about what later became the most popular slogan of Jana Sangh. The slogan 'One Country, One Nation and One Culture' became the defining feature of Jana Sangh ideology and gave it a unique identity in the national politics. By 'One Country' the party tried to convey the message, 'The whole of Bharatvarsha, from the Himalayas to Kanya Kumari, is and has been, through the ages, a living organic whole geographically, culturally and historically...economically, politically, as well as internationally, United India is essential. It is not a communal question at all'. For it 'One Nation' meant India being an ancient nation, 'Bharatiya nationalism, therefore, must naturally be based on undivided allegiance to Bharat as a whole and her great and ancient culture which distinguishes her from other lands.'[47] The other fundamental

---

[45]*Policies and Manifestos*, Party Document, vol. 1, Bharatiya Jana Sangh 1952–1980, Bharatiya Janata Party, 2005, p. 297.
[46]Ibid, p. 283.
[47]Ibid, p. 284.

of Jana Sangh, 'One Culture', sums up the understanding of the party about Indian culture and its roots in following terms:

> Unity in diversity has been the characteristic feature of Bharatiya culture which is a synthesis of different regional, local and tribal growths, natural in such a vast country. It has never been tied to the strings of any particular dogma or creed. All the creeds that form the commonwealth of Bharatiya Rashtra have their share in the stream of Bharatiya culture which has flown down from the Vedas in an unbroken continuity absorbing and assimilating contributions made by different peoples, creeds and cultures that came in touch with it in the course of history, in such a way as to make them undistinguishable part and parcel of the main current.[48]

It further distances itself from the idea of composite culture which was sought to be made the hallmark of Nehruism in the country by clearly saying that the Bharatiya culture is one and indivisible. Therefore, any talk of composite culture is illogical, unrealistic and dangerous as it tends to weaken national unity and encourage fissiparous tendencies.

The policies of Nehru were seen to be compromising on the issues of national interests and he was seen to be pursuing minority politics and appeasement of the Muslims. Jana Sangh differed from Nehru on the ground that India was neither a nation in making nor represented a composite culture; rather Indian nationalism had ancient roots and there was underlying unity in diversity which was the hallmark of Indian culture. Dr Syama Prasad Mookerjee, in his presidential address at the formation of Jana Sangh, addressed this question directly when he said:

> The Congress in its anxiety to maintain the secular character of Bharat has continued a suicidal policy of appeasement of

---

[48]Ibid, p. 284.

Muslims and some of its leaders, specially the Prime Minister taken, have special delight in outraging Hindu feelings and sentiments, and sometimes attacking Sikhs also. One may remain a good Hindu, Sikh, Buddhist, Christian or even Muslim and yet be a staunch Indian devoted to the highest national cause.[49]

MOVEMENTS ON NATIONAL ISSUES

Bharatiya Jana Sangh built its base on the basis of its ideological strength and movements on national issues. The party, while remaining committed to its principle of unflinching faith in nationalism, launched movements from time to time to oppose the Congress policies which appeared to be too compromising and weak. The movement for the complete integration of Jammu & Kashmir, liberation of Goa, mass movement against the transfer of Berubari and the demonstration against Kutch Agreement not only helped Jana Sangh to build its mass base, but also established it as a nationalist political party. Bharatiya Jana Sangh played a very effective role during Indo-China War in 1962 and staunchly opposed the policies of Nehru.

A movement under the leadership of Dr Syama Prasad Mookerjee on the issue of Kashmir and national integration was started which opposed the grant of special status to Kashmir under Article 370. The movement was started with the slogan, '*Ek Desh me do vidhan, do pradhan, do nishan, nahi challenge*' (In one country two constitutions, two heads and two emblems will not be accepted). There was a condition that anyone entering Jammu & Kashmir from rest of India was required to get an entry permit. Under this condition even the president of India had to get a permit before

---

[49]Mathur, J.P., *History of Bharatiya Jana Sangh*, Bharatiya Janata Party, vol. 6, 2006. pp. 94–95.

entering the state. It was opposed by Jana Sangh, and Dr Syama Prasad Mookerjee decided to enter Jammu & Kashmir without a permit. Leading the movement, he entered the state on 11 May 1953. The dictatorial approach of Nehru led to the arrest of Dr Syama Prasad Mookerjee who was jailed in Kashmir, where he died under mysterious circumstances on 23 June 1953. The responsibility to build the newly-born political party came on the able shoulders of Pandit Deendayal Upadhyaya.

Pt Deendayal Upadhyaya, who was earlier made general secretary of the party, played a crucial role until his death in leading the party by building its organization and ideological edifice. At the time of Kashmir movement, he played a very important role in organizing the volunteers, and brought out a full issue of *Panchjanya* on Kashmir. He wrote:

> Maharaja Hari Singh signed the instrument of Accession for making the state an integral part of India. Jammu & Kashmir, therefore, became a part of the country and any aggression on the state was an aggression on India...our fault was that we considered the aggression by Pakistan as an attack on Kashmir, and not on India.[50]

He raised the entire Kashmir problem in the context of the principles on which Indian nationhood stood. Saying that Kashmir had become the touchstone of India's secularism, he opposed the autonomy of Kashmir as separatism. He argued:

> The founders of Pakistan have based their premise on Islamic nationhood and that is why, because of Kashmir's majority Muslim population, they claim a right to it. The day they give up this basic premise, the rationale of their two-nation theory

---

[50]Sharma, Mahesh Chandra, *Pandit Deendayal Upadhyaya*, Publication Division, Ministry of Information & Broadcasting, Government of India, New Delhi, 2004, p. 41.

will fall apart... But India does not subscribe to this two-nation theory and never has subscribed to it in the past. If India's partition was based on the two-nation theory, there would be no place for Muslims in the country... We shall be dealing a blow to our nationhood if we accept Pakistan's claim over Kashmir...We were wrong in accepting plebiscite in principle to elicit the views of the population there. Unfortunately, Pakistan is still sticking to the same stand.[51]

Goa Liberation Movement

In the inaugural session of Jana Sangh held in Kanpur in 1952, Pt Deendayal Upadhyaya moved a resolution for getting liberation of Goa, Daman & Diu from Portuguese, and Pondicherry from French colonialism. It was further followed by organizing a mass awakening programme on 2 May 1954 all over the country. Thereafter, Goa Liberation week was organized from 9 December to 16 December 1954. On the death anniversary of Dr Syama Prasad Mookerjee on 21 June 1955, Jana Sangh National Secretary Jagannath Joshi led a batch of hundred satyagrahis to Goa to offer satyagraha. While Socialist Party participated in this satyagraha, Congress remained aloof and refused to become part of the ongoing liberation movement there. Jagannath Joshi said that without the liberation of Goa the independence of India is incomplete. In an article titled 'Goa, Satyagraha and Congress' he wrote:

> The movement for the liberation of Goa is gaining strength. All the political parties in India are sending volunteers to offer satyagraha there... The Congress has just decided to stay away from this movement. Not only this, the Congress has, on its part, banned participation in the satyagraha there... The basis of this move is to consider the Goans as separate from

---

[51]Ibid.

other Indian citizens... This is an all-India movement... The Congress viewpoint is that this movement for the liberation of Goa is at the same level as the ones being carried out in Algeria and Tunisia to which it has lent principled support and then kept quiet thereafter. In reality, the liberation of Goa is essential to complete India's independence.[52]

The double standard on Goa issue was exposed again when Nehru, as India's prime minister, chose to remain silent over the issue in the Asian Nation's Conference held in Bandung, while Congress as a political party passed a resolution urging the participating nations to support the move. Pt Deendayal Upadhyaya wrote, 'All-India Congress Committee should have had the courage to take the Prime Minister to task on the issue for ignoring its resolution.'[53] Goa was finally liberated through a military action in 1961.

Berubari Movement

The decision of Nehru to handover the Union Territory of Berubari to Pakistan while settling its border with Pakistan, concerning West Bengal, Assam and Tripura, received flaks from West Bengal legislative assembly which passed a unanimous resolution against it, and the Supreme Court called it unconstitutional. What was most shocking was the manner the Nehru-Noon Pact was signed between India's Prime Minister Jawaharlal Nehru and Pakistan's Prime Minister Sir Feroz Khan Noon in 1958. The people of India came to know about this only when Pakistan announced it in its parliament. Jana Sangh was in the forefront of raising this issue, and was able to convert it into a national issue. The government averted the Supreme Court ruling by bringing an amendment in the existing provisions of the Constitution. A huge demonstration was organized in front of Lok Sabha under the leadership of Pt

---

[52]Ibid, p. 44.
[53]Ibid, p. 44.

Deendayal Upadhyaya, but Nehru remained adamant and public opposition was forcefully crushed; Berubari was transferred to Pakistan.

The following analysis of the Jana Sangh regarding this issue is worth mentioning:

> In 1958, Pakistan kept firing relentlessly into Indian territory in the Cooch Behar district of Assam and the border areas of Tripura. It occupied the Tukergram village in Assam and some villages in Tripura. It was in this relation that a meeting of secretaries was called in Pakistan but it was unsuccessful. Later, the prime ministers of India and Pakistan also met. As a result, Nehru-Noon agreement was reached between the two countries on 10th of September, 1958. In this agreement the villages of Assam and Tripura were not even mentioned. They were allowed to remain in the illegal occupation of Pakistan. This was really bad but the prime minister did something even worse. He declared status quo and gave Pakistan the permission to raise the issue from scratch. He gave permission to Pakistan to make claim on areas on which there was no dispute since the Partition. A swap between the two countries was decided upon regarding areas such as the coastal area of the Ikshamati River in the 24 Pargana district and the Berubari Union area of the Jalpaiguri district, and the enclaves and exclaves of the Cooch Behar district. India stood to lose territorially in this agreement. All of this was hidden from the general public in the Nehru-Noon agreement. These issues became public when Pakistan's Prime Minister Sir Feroz Khan Noon declared about it in the Parliament of Pakistan.[54]

The people of West Bengal opposed this deal tooth and nail. Jana Sangh started a nation-wide movement against this deal. The Vidhan

---

[54]Ibid, p. 45.

Sabha and Vidhan Parishad of West Bengal passed the resolution against this deal unanimously. Chief Minister Vidhan Chandra Rai said in the Vidhan Sabha, 'The pact has been signed without the consent of the people of West Bengal.'[55]

Under pressure from the public, the President sent the issue of Berubari Union exchange to the Supreme Court for commendation. After analyzing all aspects of the issue, the Supreme Court gave a unanimous decision: 'In the present circumstances it is unconstitutional to hand over a part of India to another country.'[56]

The government then presented an amendment bill in the Parliament. Jana Sangh declared a massive protest under the leadership of Deendayal Upadhyaya in front of the Lok Sabha. However, on the strength of their majority in the Lok Sabha, the government got this bill passed in the House. Just a few weeks later, 'A few days thereafter the Chinese aggression took place and the country was placed under Emergency. Pakistan entered into an alliance with China in order to spite India. Hopes ran high among the people that India would nullify its pact with Pakistan over the transfer of Berubari. But surprisingly, measures to initiate the transfer were initiated and all protests were suppressed through police lathicharge and largescale arrests.'[57]

The decision of Nehru government hurt Deendayal deeply. Criticizing Nehru, he said, 'Pandit Nehru may be a dictator, but we do not think that he can be so callous and heartless as to completely ignore public sentiment.'[58]

The situations today are such that he seems to be the creator of India's destiny. This situation is dangerous for those who value democracy. It is dangerous even for Pandit Nehru.'

---

[55]Ibid, p. 46.
[56]Ibid, p. 46.
[57]Ibid, p. 46.
[58]Ibid, p. 47.

Opposition to Kutch Agreement

Prime Minister Lal Bahadur Shastri responded befittingly to the aggression by Pakistan on Indian borders. He was not willing to compromise in the area of national security, and was eager to teach Pakistan a lesson for its misadventures. Indian army responded strongly to the Pakistan aggression in Rann of Kutch. Deendayal Upadhyaya wrote in his article about the entire incident in detail:

> In February 1965, Pakistan Border Police started infiltration in the Rann of Kutch. On 17th March, Pakistan Rangers occupied Kanjarkot, 1300 yards inside Indian Territory. They kept doing this. On 25th of March, they occupied Dingh where the Indian Border Security Force had to retreat for 6 miles up to Vingokot... Pakistan marched forward in Kutch and on 9th April with heavy cannon fire and a huge army it attacked Sardan Post and Vingokot. Till now Indian government had left the security of borders to the Border Security Force. However, the public opinion in India was agitated against the present arrangement. As a result, the Army was given the task for protecting Kutch. The Army started pushing back the Pakistanis back to their country. As a result, on 14th April, 1965 Pakistan declared ceasefire and started talking about solving disputes by negotiations. India dismissed it by saying that there is no dispute over the Rann of Kutch. Hence, until and unless Pakistan retreats from Kanjarkot and all of the areas occupied by its Army, there will be no ceasefire.[59]

On 24 April 1965, Pakistan attacked Indian Border Post Point 84. This attack also used the American tanks, which was against the agreement with America. India brought this fact to the attention of America, but it did not pay any attention towards this breach. This increased the confidence of Pakistan even further and later

---

[59]Ibid, p. 47.

on it openly used American weapons in the war.

As soon as Indian Army prepared for embattlement against the enemy, British Prime Minister Harold Wilson appealed and a ceasefire was accepted, and later on in a meeting of Commonwealth Prime Ministers, as a result of the unofficial talks with Pakistan, it was decided to hand over the resolution of the Kutch dispute to an international jury.

This was the Kutch Agreement between India and Pakistan. While the decision of Shastri to not accept ceasefire before Pakistan returns the occupied land to India was commended by Deendayal Upadhyaya, he strongly opposed the agreement arrived at between the two countries.

A nationwide campaign was launched by Jana Sangh against Kutch Agreement to raise awareness among the people. A huge protest was organized on 16 August 1965 under the leadership of Shri Bachhraj Vyas and Pandit Deendayal Upadhyaya in front of the Parliament. Media reported the number of protestors to be about five lakhs. It was a huge rally which was enough to stir the conscience of the nation. It resulted in cancellation of the meeting of the foreign ministers of India and Pakistan that was to happen on 20 August 1965. Jana Sangh congratulated the people for rising to the occasion and making the Kutch Agreement ineffective.

INDO-PAK WAR OF 1965 AND THE TASHKENT DECLARATION

This was a new experience for Pakistan. So far, with the help of agreements and international pressure, it always had the upper hand in dealings with India. Due to the cancellation of the 20 August meeting, the Kutch Agreement was practically rendered useless. Pakistan tried to foment a big internal revolt in Kashmir by sending infiltrators, but the Indian Army foiled those attempts and occupied those areas of Pakistan-occupied Kashmir from where most of the infiltrators entered. On 25 August, Indian Army occupied all points from where the infiltrators came in. It declared ceasefire only after crossing the boundary and occupied Kargil peak and Hazipir valley.

On 1 September 1965, Pakistan attacked the Chhamb border region with heavy artillery and a great number of soldiers. It had become clear that Pakistan was preparing for a large-scale war. On 5 September, Pakistan attacked Amritsar with its air force. On 6 September Indian Army proceeded for Lahore and Sialkot. Deendayal Upadhyaya believed that the policy for which the Jana Sangh was agitating started that day.

On 6 September, Lal Bahadur Shastri called an all-party meeting in which Deendayal Upadhyaya and Sarsanghchalak Guruji Golwalkar were also invited. Preparing for war, Jana Sangh and Sangh were acting as one unit. They assured the government every kind of support. Deendayal Upadhyaya described those days of war in these proud and elated words:

> The twenty-two days period of war with Pakistan was a time of pride in the history of independent India. Indian administration decided to take a bold and courageous step. The Army and general public helped in implementing that decision with enthusiasm, hard work, patience, skill and courage. The country came to know about its strengths and weaknesses on this occasion. It also came to know who was a friend and who was an enemy. Its self-dependence and self-respect also increased. Its reverie ended and the country started walking on solid ground again. Its desire to achieve greater goals strengthened. The ideology of Bharatiya Jana Sangh started becoming the ideology of the country.[60]

The United Nations demanded a ceasefire in the name of peace. But India declined ceasefire until Pakistani Army remained on Indian

---

[60]Ibid.

soil. In 1949 too, India had declared ceasefire at the behest of the UN, but for sixteen years Pakistan occupied Indian territory, and the UN said and did nothing. Bharatiya Jana Sangh kept up the public pressure so that India does not declare ceasefire without completely freeing occupied Kashmir. A spirit of battle had pervaded throughout India.

At the behest of the Russian Prime Minister, a ceasefire was declared on 17 September 1965 and the prime ministers of India and Pakistan decided to hold a summit in Tashkent, mediated by the Soviet Union. Deendayal Upadhyaya opposed this declaration. Guruji Golwalkar gave many lectures across the country, repeating the slogan, 'Shri Shastri, do not go to Tashkent.' But no one could fight with fate. On 10 January 1967, Indian Prime Minister Lal Bahadur Shastri and Pakistani President Mohammed Ayub Khan signed the Tashkent Declaration. That night Prime Minister Lal Bahadur Shastri mysteriously died due to cardiac arrest. The announcement said, 'Indian Prime Minister and Pakistani President agreed that the armed soldiers of both the countries will return to their pre 5 August 1965 positions. This will not be done after the date of 25 February 1966 (which means the withdrawal of soldiers will be done before this date). Both the sides will respect ceasefire on the line of control.'[61]

Hence the Indian land in Kashmir that had been liberated by the Army was to be reverted back to Pakistan. If Shastri had come back to India alive, Jana Sangh would have welcomed him with black flags, however his martyrdom changed things. Deendayal Upadhyaya wrote the book, *Vishwasghat* (Betrayal) on the Tashkent Declaration. He demanded for repealing the Tashkent Declaration. He was sad at the fact that despite so much sacrifice and national enthusiasm, Pakistani aggression on Indian land could not be put to an end. Lal Bahadur Shastri was declared by Deendayal Upadhyaya as a 'National

---

[61]Tashkent Declaration, 1965.

Hero' during the war. However, in view of Tashkent Declaration, Shastri, in relation to the slogan '*Jai Jawan, Jai Kisan*', said:

> We forgot the slogan of Jai Jawan at Tashkent and as soon as we got the Americal wheat, we forgot even the other part of the slogan, Jai Kisan. This is not desirable. We cannot get foreign aid without strings.[62]

Jana Sangh resolution passed on 15 January 1965 said, 'The Tashkent Declaration...has caused deep disappointment in the country. The Declaration is no assurance of stable or real peace between India and Pakistan... It was expected that at Tashkent parleys, India would seek to secure the complete vacation of Pakistan's aggression in Kashmir. But far from doing this, India has agreed to withdraw to the '5th August line'. Thus, we would be quitting areas which are legally and constitutionally an integral part of Indian territory and which have been liberated from Pakistan's clutches by our brave jawans at a heavy price. This decision also goes counter to the solemn assurances given by the people.'

NATIONWIDE MOVEMENT FOR COW-SLAUGHTER BAN

A nationwide movement started from 1962 to 1967 demanding ban on cow slaughter across the country in accordance with the Directive Principle of the Constitution. On 5 September 1966, a huge demonstration was held in front of the parliament where Prabhudatta Brahmachari, Jain Muni Sushil Kumar and Shankaracharya of Puri went on a fast, while Sarvadaliya Goraksha Maha-abhiyan Samiti was set up. Jana Sangh participated in this movement with full force and in its Central Working Committee, held in Nagpur on 2 November 1966, it resolved:

---

[62]Sharma, Mahesh Chandra, *Pandit Deendayal Upadhyaya*, Publication Division, Ministry of Information & Broadcasting, Government of India, New Delhi, 2004, p. 51

The cow is a point of honour for India. In Indian history, there has been a ban on cow-slaughter not only during ancient days but also during the Mughal period in the reign of Akbar. A demand for a ban on cow-slaughter had also been prominent during the freedom struggle against the British and leaders had told the people that an end to British rule was necessary for cow-protection. It is a matter of regret that after attaining Independence the Congress government did not keep this promise. On the other hand, it has always avoided this subject on some pretext or the other. Immediately on attaining Independence an assurance was given that there would be a constitutional ban on cow-slaughter. But the constitution merely mentions it in Article 48 in the Directive Principles of state policy. The hope was held out that a law would soon be made in accordance with this directive. When such a law was demanded after nation-wide collection of record signatures in 1952, the matter was passed on into the laps of the State Governments.[63]

A huge demonstration of about more than 1,25,000 people was held on 7 November 1967. The demonstration was fired upon by police, resulting in the death of many people. Many Jana Sangh leaders, including L.K. Advani, V.K. Malhotra, Om Prakash Tyagi, Vasant Rao Oak, Balraj Madhok and Hansraj Gupta were arrested; they were released later. Many sadhus languished in jail for a longtime.

PERFORMANCE IN ELECTIONS

The newly-formed party had to face general elections within two months of its formation. It was a very challenging time for the newly-formed party. In the elections, the party fielded 93 candidates

---

[63]Mathur, J.P., *History of Bharatiya Jana Sangh*, Bharatiya Janata Party, vol. 6, 2006, p. 273.

for Lok Sabha and 725 candidates for legislative assemblies. It won 4 Lok Sabha seats, 2 from West Bengal and 2 from Rajasthan. Dr Syama Prasad Mookerjee was elected from Midnapur, West Bengal. Out of the 725 assembly seats it contested, it could win only 35 seats. As a new party, Jana Sangh lacked experience and mass contact, and its organizational structure was in a very nascent stage. The party also struggled to arrange resources. The only solace for the party was that it garnered 3.06 per cent of the popular votes and was thus recognized as a national party.

After the death of Dr Syama Prasad Mookerjee, Jana Sangh had no leader of national stature and it also had to face internal problems. In 1957 Jana Sangh contested 130 seats in Lok Sabha and 606 in legislative assemblies. The campaign was vicious and Jana Sangh was targeted as communal by Congress, communists and Muslim League, who spoke in single voice. Craig Baxter in his book *The Jana Sangh: A Biography of an Indian Political Party* observed:

> The party (Jana Sangh) was again branded by its opponents as communal. The Congress, particularly Nehru, worked hard against the Jana Sangh. The PSP and CPI also bore down hard on the Jana Sangh... It was again a rough campaign and much was said in the heat of the battle, which would be forgotten, if not regretted, after the elections were over. But the secularist and socialist Congress of Nehru again feared the Hindu parties of the right more than the parties of the left.[64]

Contrary to the expectations of those opposed to Jana Sangh, results were very encouraging for the new party which was led by young people. Its popular votes almost doubled to 5.93 per cent since the 1952 elections and it won 4 Lok Sabha seats. It won 2 seats each from Uttar Pradesh and Maharashtra where the party contested 61 and 7 seats, respectively. In Uttar Pradesh, its vote share doubled

---

[64]Ibid, p. 217.

from 7.29 per cent to 17.79 per cent. Atal Bihari Vajpayee, who contested three seats, won Balrampur Lok Sabha seat. Jana Sangh could not win any seat in other states, but its vote share showed a remarkable surge, for instance in Madhya Pradesh, where its vote share increased from 5.92 per cent to 13.96 per cent; in Haryana from 7.41 per cent to 22.75 per cent; in Punjab from 3.05 per cent to 13.32 per cent; in Rajasthan from 3.67 per cent to 11.01 per cent; and in Delhi it got 25.92 per cent.

In assemblies, Jana Sangh had contested 606 seats and won 51. It improved its vote share from 2.67 per cent to 4.03 per cent, making substantial gains in states like Uttar Pradesh, Madhya Pradesh, Rajasthan, Punjab and Haryana. In Uttar Pradesh it won 17 out of 235 seats it contested. In Rajasthan it won 6 seats out of 47 it contested, in Madhya Pradesh it won 10 out of 127 seats it contested and in Maharashtra it won 4 out of 18 it contested. In Jammu & Kashmir it won 5 seats out of 22 seats with 24.63 per cent votes and in Haryana it won 4 seats with 12.02 per cent of the popular votes. In Assam, Madras and Orissa it did not put any candidates, and the results were not encouraging in Bihar, Karnataka, West Bengal and Gujarat.

In his annual report in the Sixth Annual Session of the party held in Ambala from 4–6 April 1958, Pt Deendayal Upadhyaya said:

> After the death of Dr Syama Prasad Mookerjee, it was presumed in the political circle that Jana Sangh would now be finished. We have fought against this presumption for the last five years. Now the results of the second General Elections have proved that Jana Sangh is not only alive but progressing. This would never have happened had we not been true to our principles and our leader.[65]

The party had great expectations from the 1962 elections as ten

---

[65]Ibid, p. 219.

years of its existence had given it time to expand and consolidate. Jana Sangh decided to go alone this time, as opposed to the 1957 general elections where it had local seat adjustments with parties like Ram Rajya Parishad and Hindu Mahasabha. Elections were held on 494 Lok Sabha seats and for all state assemblies, except Kerala and Orissa where elections had already taken place in 1960 and 1961, respectively. Jana Sangh contested 198 Lok Sabha seats and 1,140 assembly seats. It contested 377 assembly seats out of 430 seats and 195 of 288 seats in Madhya Pradesh. When the results were declared, Jana Sangh won 14 Lok Sabha seats in contrast to 4 in 1957, and 116 assembly seats in contrast to 51 in 1957 elections. The vote share in Lok Sabha increased from 5.93 per cent in 1957 to 6.44 per cent in 1962 and in assembly from 4.03 per cent to 6.07 per cent. Although it was a major gain from the last elections, yet the expectations were very high and most of its leaders who were elected last time, including Atal Bihari Vajpayee, lost the elections. In Uttar Pradesh and Madhya Pradesh, the party became 'official Opposition party' with 49 and 41 seats, respectively. It was a big leap as in 1957 Jana Sangh had only 17 members in Uttar Pradesh and 10 in Madhya Pradesh assemblies. The election also saw a sharp rise in vote share of the party, but the party could not win as many seats owing to division of votes between it, the Swatantra Party, Hindu Mahasabha and Ram Rajya Parishad. A case in point was the defeat of Atal Bihari Vajpeyee who lost by 2,000 votes, whereas Swatantra Party candidate got 20,000 votes and Hindu Mahasabha candidate garnered 5,000 votes. Pt Deendayal Upadhyaya, while analyzing the results said:

> The Swatantara Party entered into alliance with practically every party other than the Congress, including the Akali Dal, Dravida Munnetra Kazhagam and the communists. Hindu Mahasabha and Ram Rajya Parishad entered into a compromise and contested the elections. The Republican

Party contested with two groups—Praja Socialist Party supporting Vidarbha and the communists. In Uttar Pradesh there was an agreement between the old Muslim League elements and the Republican Party. The Congress tried to enter into an alliance with the Jharkhand Party, but it was not successful... The Bharatiya Jana Sangh and the Socialist Party are the only parties that contested the elections on the basis of their policies.[66]

He further said that Jana Sangh was the party of the future as other political parties were on decline and Jana Sangh was supposed to fulfil a historic mission. He said:

The Congress is disintegrating rapidly. Defeated in their bastions, the communists have slightly increased their tally by picking up in other parts of the country. The beginning of the end of Praja Socialist Party has started...The Bharatiya Jana Sangh has taken a step forward, but it still lags behind in fulfilling the historic mission with which it was formed.[67]

1967 ELECTIONS

For the first time in 1967, the Congress monopoly over power was breached due to the initiatives taken by Bharatiya Jana Sangh and Pt Deendayal Upadhyaya. Congress was defeated in assembly elections in various states. Pt Deendayal Uapdhyaya never believed in the politics of convenience and opportunistic alliances, and he was also opposed to the idea of political untouchability. The 1963 by-elections, in which Deendayal Upadhyaya and Ram Manohar

---

[66]Sharma, Mahesh Chandra, *Pandit Deendayal Upadhyaya*, Publication Division, Ministry of Information & Broadcasting, Government of India, New Delhi, 2004, p. 143..
[67]Ibid.

Lohia contested in a joint platform against Congress, created an atmosphere of goodwill between the Jana Sangh and Samyukta Socialist Party workers. The goodwill was further strengthened by the Deendayal-Lohia joint statement that was issued on 12 April 1964. It was issued in the context of large scale riots in East Pakistan and increasing influx of Hindus and other minorities to India. The statement read:

> It is our firm conviction that guaranteeing the protection of the life and property of Hindus and other minorities in Pakistan is the responsibility of the Government of India. To take a nice legalistic view about the matter that Hindus in Pakistan are Pakistan nationals would be dangerous and can only result in killings and reprisals in the two countries, in greater of lesser measure. When the Government of India fails to fulfil this obligation towards the minorities in Pakistan, the people understandably become indignant. Our appeal to the people is that this indignation should be directed against the Government and should in no case be given vent against the Indian Muslims. If the latter things happen, it only provides Government with a cloak to cover its own inertia and failure, and an opportunity to malign the people and repress them.[68]

Such statements brought both the leaders closer. However, this could not lead to the formation of an anti-Congress front by both the parties, as they contested the 1967 elections separately. But Jana Sangh was able to reach an understanding with Swatantra Party. Electoral understanding with Swatantra Party was reached in Gujarat, Rajasthan, Haryana, Punjab and Himachal Pradesh. In Madhya Pradesh, Jana Sangh, Swatantra Party and Rajmata, who had come out of the Congress, reached an electoral understanding,

---

[68]Mathur, J.P., *History of Bharatiya Jana Sangh*, Bharatiya Janata Party, vol. 6, 2006, pp. 275–276.

but they also fought against each other on a few seats. Jana Sangh went to polls alone in Uttar Pradesh and Bihar.

The 1967 elections proved to be a milestone in the Indian politics as Congress returned to power in the centre with majority of only 24 seats and, for the first time, lost in eight states. The performance of Jana Sangh was spectacular as its seat in Lok Sabha increased from 14 to 35 and its vote share increased from 6.44 per cent to 9.41 per cent. The party also won 261 assembly seats in comparison to 119 seats which it won in 1962. In the Lok Sabha, the party finished second in 75 constituencies and lost by a slim margin, ranging from 200 to 5000 votes in 15 constituencies. It won assembly seats in Andhra Pradesh and Karnataka for the first time and got absolute majority in Metropolitan Council and Municipal Corporation in Delhi, winning 6 out of 7 Lok Sabha seats.

The Congress lost in Madras to DMK and in Delhi to Jana Sangh. It also failed to get majority in the states of Uttar Pradesh, Rajasthan, Punjab, West Bengal and Kerala. Jana Sangh emerged the second largest party in Uttar Pradesh, Madhya Pradesh and Haryana. In Orissa, Andhra Pradesh and Gujarat, its alliance partner became the second largest party. The Central Working Committee of the Jana Sangh, while deliberating on the results, observed:

> As a result of these elections, the Congress has received a big shock. It has failed to secure a majority in eight states as well as in Delhi. At the Centre too, its majority has a very narrow margin. These elections have shown the people's great resentment and lack of confidence in the Congress. Clearly it is on the way out.[69]

The situation in the states, where no party had majority, was complex as there was no way out except the formation of coalition governments. So, India had entered the era of coalition politics for

---

[69]Ibid, p. 291.

the first time, but it was not an easy decision for Jana Sangh. While the party had ideological differences with other political parties, it was staunchly opposed to communists. There were differences of opinion within Jana Sangh on the question of participation in coalition government. The party deliberated the situation on 14 March 1967 and came out with the decision:

> Because of the defeat of the Congress and the inability of any one of the parties to secure a majority, it has become impossible in many States to form a Government unless all non-Congress parties come together. To let the Congress form a Government in such states would not only amount to flouting the people's feelings but would also strike at their self-confidence. This situation is not conducive for the development of democracy. Hence the Central Working Committee favours the inclusion of Jana Sangh MLAs in non-Congress Ministries. These members will remain in the Ministry so long as they can effectively serve the people on the basis of the principles and programmes of the Jana Sangh. The Legislative Party should maintain its organisation and work according to its Constitution.[70]

Pt Deendayal Upadhyaya, who was an ideologue as well as one of the main decision makers of the party, had to find a solution to the then prevailing ideological dilemma and the situation that was created due to a fractured mandate. Jana Sangh functioned in its ideological premise and was known for taking principled stand on various issues. There was doubt that forming a government with parties having ideological differences and with the ones whose policies it had been opposing, might not appear convincing to a section of the Jana Sangh activists and supporters. Deendayal Upadhyaya himself was against any shortcut route to power and

---

[70]Ibid, p. 291.

opposed to opportunistic alliances. He tried to resolve the question by assessing the situation on practical grounds and attempted to give a theoretical solution in the following terms:

> The Congress majority in many states came to end but except in Delhi and Madras no single party could muster majority. As a result, the era of coalition governments has come into being. The objective of these alliances is to somehow cobble a majority in order to remain in power. There is no need for any party to change its thinking or policies. Nor should they take any decision to remain together on the basis of a principled stand. This is a practical issue in the present circumstances; the various political parties preferred to form alliances to allow the imposition of President's Rule and formation of Congress Government later. These governments have been formed on the basis of such thinking and they will continue as long as there is willingness to run the administration on practical consideration.[71]

As a result, non-Congress coalition governments were formed in many states. The first coalition government was formed in Bihar; Congress had won 128 seats in the house of 318 members, while Jana Sangh had 26, SSP 68, PSP 18, CPI 24, CPI(M) 4, Swatantra Party 3 and independents 21 seats. Mahamaya Prasad Sinha came out of Congress to form Jana Kranti Dal with 26 MLAs and became the chief minister while Karpoori Thakur of SSP became deputy chief minister. Jana Sangh, which joined the government along with the communists, had two cabinet and one state minister in this government.

In Punjab, Jana Sangh had 9 seats which formed a government with Akalis, with Gurnam Singh as chief minister and Chaudhary Baldev Prakash of Jana Sangh as deputy chief minister. Republican,

---

[71]Ibid.

CPI, CPI(M), SSP and some independents were also part of this coalition government.

In Uttar Pradesh, Congress had 207 seats out of 423 seats and Chandra Bhanu Gupta of Congress was sworn in as chief minister. But Charan Singh rebelled and left Congress along with many of his supporters, and he was chosen leader by the opposition Samyukta Vidhayak Dal. He was sworn in as chief minister and Jana Sangh's Ram Prakash Gupta became deputy chief minister, and there were four cabinet and three deputy ministers from Jana Sangh.

In Haryana, although Congress had won 48 seats and had majority, and Bhagwat Dayal Sharma was sworn in as chief minister, yet there was rebellion from within and a government with Rao Birendra Singh as chief minister was formed with the outside support of Jana Sangh.

In Madhya Pradesh, too, Congress had to face rebellion. It had won 167 seats in the house of 296, and the combined opposition had a strength of 129 members. Although D.P. Mishra was elected chief minister, his government was pulled down; Govind Narayan Singh became the chief minister and Virendra Kumar Sakhlecha of Jana Sangh became deputy chief minister. Many ministers from Jana Sangh were included in the government along with SSP and PSP members.

LOK SABHA ELECTIONS—1971

After the unfortunate murder of Deendayal in 1968, the responsibility to lead Jana Sangh as its president fell on the shoulders of Atal Bihari Vajpayee. Jana Sangh entered into a pre-poll alliance with Swatantra Party, Congress (O) and Samyukta Socialist Party. Jana Sangh went to the elections on its own manifesto, mainly raising the issue of unemployment, price-rise, burden of budget on common man, vagaries of license-permit-quota raj, bureaucratic red tapism and Indira Gandhi's policies endangering the future of the nation.

While questioning the secularism of Congress in the wake of its alliance with Muslim League in Kerala, the manifesto also declared war on poverty.

Jana Sangh contested 159 seats all across India, except Manipur and Dadra and Nagar Haveli. The results were a huge disappointment for Opposition parties with Indira Gandhi romping home with 352 seats in a house of 518, winning two-third majority. The Jana Sangh could win only 22 seats, including 11 from Madhya Pradesh, 4 each from UP and Rajasthan, 2 from Bihar and 1 from Haryana. The share of popular vote also declined from 9.41 per cent in 1967 elections to 7.35 per cent. Swatantra Party could win only 9 seats while it held 44 in the outgoing house and the socialists, including PSP and SSP, could win only 5 in place of 36 seats which they held in the last house.

Jana Sangh CWC, which met on 15 March 1971 to discuss election results, besides various other things, expressed concerns over the dangers posed by two-third majority to Indira Gandhi in following words:

> There is danger also that the absolute power now given to Smt Gandhi's party may make the party even more disdainful of democratic procedures and norms than it already is. The PM's first reference after elections about Supreme Court has confirmed the people's worst fears about the ruling party wanting to denigrate and devalue the independent status of the Judiciary. All democrats inside and outside parliament must keep vigilante watch over these trends, and firmly resist all such attempts.[72]

The fears expressed then proved to be true in the years that unfolded. The events that followed led to amendment of the Constitution, excluding judiciary from scrutiny of parliament's amendments of

---

[72]Ibid, p. 314.

the Constitution amid talks of committed judiciary. All these events culminated in the imposition of Emergency over the country and muzzling of all voices of dissent, jailing of Opposition leaders, censorship over press, suspension of fundamental rights and repression of all dissent.

FORMATION OF JANATA PARTY AND MERGER OF BHARATIYA JANA SANGH

People were becoming restive under the authoritarian rule of Congress government led by Indira Gandhi. Student movement started in Bihar along with the Navnirman Movement in Gujarat. Congress chose to suppress these movements. Loknayak Jayaprakash Narayan agreed to lead the movement against the repressive Congress regime, as public unrest against the Congress government became stronger throughout the country. In 1971, 'External Emergency' provisions were brought into force in view of Indo-Pak war and Bangladesh liberation movement, which continued even after the war was over, and the situation was normalized. The demand to lift the emergency was growing stronger. The Indira-led Congress, fearing nationwide public unrest, tried to muzzle the voice of the people. On 25 June 1975, under Article 352 of the Indian Constitution, 'Internal Emergency' was imposed on the country in addition to 'External Emergency' which already was in force. All the top leaders of the Opposition were either put into house arrest or jailed. Censorship was imposed on the press. Rashtriya Swayamsevak Sangh, along with many other organizations, was banned. Thousands of activists were arrested under the draconian law 'MISA' and put into jails. The democracy was imperiled. Mass struggle started growing stronger, with underground activities playing the role of a catalyst. Increasing strength of people's movement against Emergency and growing unpopularity forced Indira Gandhi to dissolve Lok Sabha on 18 January 1977 in order to seek a fresh mandate. A new political party by the name of Janata Party was formed on the call of Jayaprakash Narayan. As there was very little time left for the elections, Janata Party could not be formed as a full-fledged political party. In the 1977 general elections, Congress was completely routed and Janata Party, along with other political formations, returned with thumping victory. As per earlier announcement, in a conference of around 5,000 delegates, Bharatiya Jana Sangh merged itself with Janata Party on 1 May 1977.

INTEGRAL HUMANISM—
HIS IDEAS AND PHILOSOPHY

*We have to undertake the task of awakening our nation's 'Virat'.
Let us go forward in this task with a sense of pride for our heritage,
with a realistic assessment of the present and a great ambition for
the future. We wish neither to make this country a shadow of some
distant past nor an imitation of Russia or America. With the support
of universal knowledge and our heritage, we shall create a Bharat
which will excel all its past glories, and will enable every citizen
in its fold to steadily progress in the development of his manifold
latent possibilities and to achieve, through a sense of unity with
the entire creation, a state even higher than that of a complete
human being; to become Narayan from 'Nar'. This is the external
divine form of our culture. This is our message to humanity at
the crossroads. May God give us strength to succeed in this task.*

—Pt Deendayal Upadhyaya
(concluding his lectures on Integral Humanism)

Pandit Deendayal Upadhyaya is remembered as a great
philosopher who, as a political activist and leader, not only
laid down the principles but also lived those principles in

his political life. A towering personality well-versed in different disciplines, he was able to give direction to national politics through his intellectual insight and deep understanding of Indian civilizational values. While his ideas and philosophy still remain relevant, his contribution as an ideologue and a guiding force for an alternative model of governance and politics continues to define and determine the course of politics in the country. Norman D. Palmer of Pennsylvania University wrote:

> Deendayal belongs to a rare breed of political thinkers; the likes of him are very few. His image as an original political thinker was gradually gaining strength. In addition to belonging to a large political party in India, Deendayal possessed a distinctive image that first attracted me to him.[73]

Pandit Deendayal Upadhyaya is widely acclaimed as the propounder of the philosophy of Integral Humanism. He never sought to follow a piecemeal approach to seek solutions for the problems afflicting the nation, rather he aspired to devise a philosophy which may herald an era of integral approach. He advocated the vision of envisaging the integral well-being of the individual, seeking to achieve a balance, cohesion and harmony between the body, mind, intellect and soul of each human being. While seeking to spiritualize the politics like Gandhi, he laid emphasis on coining the idioms of national discourse in civilizational and cultural ethos of India. He was not in favour of adopting borrowed ideas from the West for goals of national reconstruction. He never considered either capitalism or socialism a solution to problems of the human society. According to him, 'A capitalist economy first acquires power in the economic field and then enters the political field, while socialism concentrates power over all means of production in the

---

[73]Sharma, Mahesh Chandra, *Pandit Deendayal Upadhyaya*, Publication Division, Ministry of Information & Broadcasting, Government of India, New Delhi, 2004, p. 116.

hands of state. Both these systems are against democratic rights of individuals.'[74]

Deendayal was elected general secretary of Jana Sangh in its all-India session held in Kanpur, 1952. He was also credited with drafting eight of 16 resolutions which were adopted by Jana Sangh in its first all-India session. He regularly presented his ideas in the RSS meditation camps which also helped him in gradually developing his ideas on various issues of national importance. He was handpicked by Guruji Golwalkar for having a rare combination of deep ideological understanding and organizational skills. While building the organizational structure and making electoral strategies to win elections are priorities of any political party, Jana Sangh had a different agenda of creating space for nationalist politics and securing legitimacy in the larger national context. In the post-independence era, the nation was to find its way forward through various programmes and policies which were conceptualized in the context of Western thinking that supported the continuation of colonial ideas of society, culture, economy and politics. It was the responsibility of Jana Sangh to conceive ideas which were rooted in Indian civilization and culture and also in consonance with the contemporary aspirations and urge of the people. Right from the beginning, the party considered 'nationalism' as its core principle, but it required to be articulated in its various dimensions, and Indian thoughts and philosophy required to be propounded in accordance with the newly emerging perspective. It was a huge challenge as the intellectual scene was not only dominated but even monopolized by the Nehruvian-Marxist intellectuals who mostly felt inspired by the Western ideas and were completely awed by their achievements in the modern world. Deendayal took upon himself to build the ideological edifice of Jana Sangh by propounding the philosophy

---

[74]Deendayal Sansar: A complete Deendayal Reader, Centralization of Power, http://deendayalupadhyay.org/demo.html

of Integral Humanism.

In January 1964 at Vijayavada, Bharatiya Jana Sangh adopted the statement of 'Principles and Policies' in which Integral Humanism was accepted. Further, in Gwalior training camp, this line of thinking was developed from 11–15 August 1964, where the outline of the 'Principles and Policies' were presented by Deendayal. And finally, four continuous lectures were delivered from 22–25 April 1965 in Mumbai, where he expounded the philosophy of Integral Humanism. In the preface, he quoted Jagadguru Shankaracharya and Chanakya:

> One remembers two thinkers who brought about a radical change in Indian history. One is reminded of the times when Jagadguru Shankaracharya started off to put an end to the chaos prevailing in the eternal Hindu faith and the other is when, propounding the idea of republic to bring together the scattered nationalistic forces, Chanakya set off to establish an empire. Looking back on these developments, a third outline has emerged today when, inspired by foreign thought and its vague concept of a divided man, the pure and unadulterated concept of integrated humanism is being started by us.[75]

BACKGROUND OF INTEGRAL HUMANISM

Lecture I: 22 April 1965

The main challenge before India after achieving independence was to find its way forward; it had to find the direction in which it was supposed to move as a nation. There was little thinking on this line. After independence, the colonial policies and programmes

---

[75]Sharma, Mahesh Chandra, *Pandit Deendayal Upadhyaya*, Publication Division, Ministry of Information & Broadcasting, Government of India, New Delhi, 2004, p. 117.

were continuing, and aping the Western models was considered the only alternative. Before independence also, not much thought was given to this issue as the main concern then was to get freedom from the British rule. But an insight into the manner the country should move forward may be found in the writings of the great freedom fighters and the resolutions passed from time to time by different organizations. In the first lecture delivered on 22 April 1965, Deendayal said that the root of the problem was the neglect of 'self' and national identity. He said:

> It is essential that we think about our national identity. Without this identity there is no meaning of independence, nor can independence become the instrument of progress and happiness. As long as we are unaware of our national identity, we cannot recognize and develop all our potentialities. Under alien rule this identity is suppressed. That is why nations wish to remain independent so that they can progress according to their natural bent and can experience happiness in their endeavour... The basic cause of the problems facing Bharat is the neglect of its national identity.[76]

India as an ancient nation was to realize its 'self' after independence. But how? This question was still to be addressed. In his opinion, it was not possible to go a thousand years back when foreign invaders started disrupting the national life. The nation had its own mechanism to deal with the situation and managed to continue fighting for independence, while maintaining the advance of its national life. He said:

> ... it would not be rational to say that the thousand-year-old alien rule has interrupted the current of our national life so completely that from that time to this day we remained

---

[76]Deendayal Sansar: A complete Deendayal Reader webportal: http://deendayalupadhyay.org/leacture1.html

stationary and inactive. The nation has certainly put her genius to work in the changing circumstances to meet the challenges thrown at her. We have struggled to continue our life forward and to wrest independence from the aliens. The current of our national life was not interrupted but has gone on ceaselessly.[77]

While India was being subjugated and it fought for its independence, the other parts of the world made phenomenal advance. Though the Indians felt a sense of pride when they discarded Western clothes during the freedom struggle, there was a trend to blindly ape Western models, practices and values after gaining independence. Systemic representation of all things Western as superior, and subtle creation of contempt for all things Indian led to such a trend. While saying that a nation cannot make any progress without rising above the narrow sense of nationalism, he pleaded that 'thoughtless imitation of the West must be scrupulously discarded.' He said:

> The difficulty arises when we fail to discern the reasons of the spectacular advance of the West, its effects, real and apparent. This is further complicated by the fact that Britishers as representative of the West, ruled this country for a century and, during this period adopted such measures whereby in the minds of our people a contempt for things Bharatiya and respect for everything Western were subtly created. Along with the scientific advance, their way of life, manners and food habits, etc. came to this country. Not only material sciences but also their social, economic and political doctrines became our standards.[78]

While making a distinction between Western science and its economic and political doctrine, he said that West was itself at crossroads and was still not sure which path it should pursue.

---

[77]Ibid.
[78]ibid, http://deendayalupadhyay.org/leacture9.html

Attempting to transplant those doctrines without understanding the historical circumstances in which they had originated, might not be helpful for India. He said:

> There are those who consider economic and political doctrines of the West as epitome of progress, and desire to transplant the same in our country. Therefore, when we are trying to decide where we wish to take our country and how, we must also take into consideration the basis of various economic and political doctrines of the West and their present position.[79]

He questioned the efficacy of the political and economic doctrines that were conceptualized in the West for India. The birth of 'isms', like nationalism and socialism, has had huge impact on the West, which showed formation of nation-states, industrial revolution, rise of democracy, exploitation of people, socialism and Marxist idea of Dialectic Materialism and dictatorship of the proletariat. The Roman Empire fell and influence of the Catholic Church started waning. The process of emergence of nations in Europe started in the shape of different monarchies, thereby paving the way for the formation of nation-states. These nation-states later embraced democracy, while the Industrial Revolution in the meantime created a new basis for the economy, wherein factories were established. Individual labour had to shift to factories for work, leaving behind the workplace owned by them. It created a situation leading to the exploitation of individual labour, creating tension in the society. Marx's conceptualization of Dialectic Materialism and social revolution in some European countries raised question on this model of development. Countries that desisted socialism accepted the rights of workers and the concept of 'welfare state' as an ideal model of governance. He further said that the doctrines of nationalism, democracy and socialism dominated

---

[79]ibid.

the mental landscape of the political thinkers, and a section of them were also attracted by the ideas of world peace and world unity. He equated socialism with the concept of equality, but also distinguished between 'equality' and 'equability'. He further said that while all these ideas are good in themselves and reflect the higher aspirations of mankind, the real problems are that all these doctrines are incomplete. The problem got further compounded when all these doctrines were seen in opposition to each other, leading to a gap between theory and practice. He analyzed this paradox in the European context very accurately when he said:

> Nationalism poses a threat to world peace. Democracy and capitalism join hands to give a free reign of exploitation. Socialism replaced capitalism and brought with it end to democracy and individual freedom. Hence the West is faced with the task of reconciling these good ideals. They have not succeeded to this day, in this task. They have tried combinations and permutations, by emphasis on one or the other ideal. England emphasized nationalism and democracy and developed her politico-social institutions along those lines, whereas France could not adopt the same. There, democracy resulted in political instability. The British Labour party wanted to reconcile socialism with democracy but people have raised doubts whether democracy will survive if socialism gains strength. Hence the labour party no longer supports socialism as strongly as the Marxist doctrines advocate. If socialism has been diluted considerably, Hitler and Mussolini have adopted nationalist-cum-socialism and buried democracy. In the end socialism also became a tool for their nationalism which posed a great threat to world peace and unity.[80]

---

[80]Ibid.

West was itself at crossroads. In such circumstances, he said, the West was unable to guide India, rather India should think about its role in resolving this Western paradox. While acknowledging the contribution of the West in the field of science and technology, Deendayal was always doubtful about its economic and political doctrines, which according to him, were unable to provide complete solution to mankind. His vision was influenced by the understanding of Swami Vivekanand and Maharishi Aurobindo. He had great respect for Mahatma Gandhi's *Hind Swaraj*, Bal Gangadhar Tilak's *Geeta Rahasya* and even quoted Vinoba Bhave in his writings. His ideas represented a confident India which was ready to accept challenges and even willing to shoulder the responsibilities of the world. In his opinion, blind aping of the West was going to complicate the situation as such a trend would not lead the country anywhere. He said:

> In this era of adulteration, instead of adulterating ideas we must, on the contrary, scrutinize and improve upon them wherever possible before accepting them. Rather than being a burden on the world, we must attempt to resolve, if possible, the problems facing the world.[81]

Lecture II: 23 April 1965

The main question before India after independence was how to move forward. What direction the nation should take for its progress and solution of political, economic and social problems. India being an ancient nation and a living civilization, had its own unique culture that celebrated plurality and diversity. The advance of the Western world and modernity fascinated India, leading to a debate between ancient and modern ideas. In his second lecture on 23 April 1965, he tried to focus on this dilemma. He said:

---

[81]Ibid.

There are some who suggest that we must go back to the position when we lost our independence and proceed from there. On the other hand, there are people who would like to discard all that has originated here in Bharat and are not ready to think about it. They seem to think that Western life and thoughts are the last word in progress and all of it should be imported here if we are to develop. Both these lines of thought are incorrect, though they do represent partial truths and it will not be proper to discard them altogether. Those who advocate starting from where we left off a thousand years ago, forget that whether it may or may not be desirable, it is definitely impossible. The flow of time cannot be reversed.[82]

He said that in the past, when the reins of India was in the hands of foreigners, the nation did not accept everything that was imposed on it passively, but created its own mechanisms to meet the challenges and adapted to the situation by reshaping the national life. The past cannot be disowned, nor can the fact be ignored that the last one thousand years of slavery led us to find ways to negotiate with the challenges effectively. While past cannot be disowned, the ideas that originated in the foreign countries are also not universal as they, too, are the product of their own time and situations, and many of them are outdated. He had an interesting observation when he said, 'It is indeed surprising that those who claim to reform the society by removing dead traditions,[83] themselves fall prey to some outdated foreign traditions.' But at the same time, he also said that human knowledge is a common property and should not be ignored completely. He said:

On the other hand it needs to be realized that not all the thoughts and principles that have sprung up elsewhere are

---

[82]ibid, http://deendayalupadhyay.org/leacture2.html
[83]Ibid.

necessarily local in space and time. The response of human beings in a particular place, time and social atmosphere may, and does, in many cases have relation and use to other human beings elsewhere and at other times. Therefore to ignore altogether the developments in other societies, past or present, is certainly unwise. Whatever truths these developments contain must be taken note of and accepted. The rest must be scrupulously avoided. While absorbing the wisdom of other societies it is only proper that we avoid their mistakes or perversities. Even their wisdom should be adapted to our particular circumstances. In brief, we must absorb the knowledge and gains of the entire humanity so far as eternal principles and truths are concerned. Of these, the ones that originated in our midst have to be clarified and adapted to changed times and those that we take from other societies have to be adapted to our conditions.[84]

While the Western political thought originated in particular situations and times, the problem in reconciling these ideas led to conflicts in the society. The idea of nationalism, democracy and socialism were seen incomplete in practice and even in mutual conflict. The sustenance of life and progress of humankind depends on its capacity to mould its nature towards attainment of social goals and it's possible through mutual cooperation. This is what the term 'culture' stands for, while conflict gives way to 'perversion'. Mutual conflict is not a sign of culture but of regression and degradation. He believed that if Bharatiya culture had the ability to find the idea of unity from within its manifest diversities, and if Western political principles, which were the product of 'revolution in human thought, and social conflict', could find unity and harmony from within, then the national life would have added advantages to it. He further explained his ideas when he said:

---

[84]Ibid.

The first characteristic of Bharatiya culture is that it looks upon life as an integrated whole. It has an integrated view point. To think in parts may be proper for a specialist but it is not useful from the practical standpoint. The confusion in the West arises primarily from its tendency to think of life in sections and then to attempt to put them together by patchwork. We do admit that there is diversity and plurality in life but we have always attempted to discover the unity behind them. This attempt is thoroughly scientific. The scientists always attempt to discover order in the apparent disorder in the universe, to find out the principles governing the universe and frame practical rules on the basis of these principles. Chemists discovered that a few elements comprise the entire physical world. Physicists went one step further and showed that even these elements consist only of energy. Today we know that the entire universe is only a form of energy.[85]

While stressing that 'an integrated life is the foundation and the principle underlying this culture as well as its aims and ideals',[86] he said that in our culture, life has been seen as an integrated whole not only in social or collective life, but in individual life as well. An individual is made of body, mind, intelligence and soul which, although being separate components, cannot be considered separately but as an integrated whole. He said the problem in the West was that they considered themselves separate, and hence reached to faulty conclusions. When they saw man as a 'political animal', they ignored the other aspects and attended to his political aspirations giving him voting rights and making him the king. He summed up the problem very interestingly in the following words,

---

[85]Ibid.
[86]Ibid, http://deendayalupadhyay.org/leacture10.html

They wondered, 'Now that you have voting right, you are the king. Why need you worry?' But man replied, 'What shall I do with the state if I do not get any food? I have no use of this voting right. I want bread first.' Then came Karl Marx and said, 'Yes, bread is the most important thing. The state belongs to the "haves". So let us fight for bread.' He saw man as primarily made up of body, wanting bread. But those who followed the path shown by Karl Marx came to realize that they had neither bread nor voting-right.[87]

At the opposite end there is the USA. There is both bread as well as voting right. Even so there is lack of peace and happiness. The USA has the highest list of suicides, mental patients and persons using tranquilizers to get sleep. People are puzzled as to the cause of this new situation. Man obtained bread, he got his voting right, still there is no peace, no happiness. Now they want back their peaceful sleep. Sound and undisturbed sleep is a scarce commodity in the present-day America. Those who think deeply realize that there is a basic mistake somewhere, whereby even after acquiring all the good things of life, they are not happy.

He further clarified that contrary to the impression that Indian thought only centres around salvation of the soul, the reality is that it considers body, mind, intellect and soul as an integrated whole. He said that the upanishads clearly state that a weakling cannot realize the self. Along with the thinking about the individual in terms of body, intellect, mind and soul as an integrated whole, he also suggested fourfold responsibilities. He said:

The fundamental difference between our position and that of the West is that whereas they have regarded body and satisfaction of its desires as the aim, we regard the body as an instrument for achieving our aims. We have recognized the

---

[87]Ibid.

importance of the body only in this light. The satisfaction of our bodily needs is necessary, but we don't consider this to be the sole aim of all our efforts. Here in Bharat, we have placed before ourselves the ideal of the fourfold responsibilities, of catering to the needs of body, mind, intellect and soul with a view of achieving the integrated progress of man. Dharma, Artha, Kama and Moksha are the four kinds of human effort. Purushartha means efforts which befit a man. The longings for Dharma, Artha, Kama and Moksha are inborn in man. Of these four efforts too, we have thought in an integrated way.[88]

He said that Dharma, Artha, Kama and Moksha are inter-related and influence each other. He described these concepts as, 'Artha includes what is known as political and economic policies. In ancient India, it used to include justice and punishment also. Kama relates to the satisfaction of various natural desires. Dharma defines a set of rules to regulate the social activity. In order to progress in an integral and harmonious way, one should attain not only Kama and Artha, but also Moksha eventually.'[89] Dharma is of primary importance but one should bear in mind that in the absence of Artha, Dharma cannot be practised. Similarly, Artha and Kama may be achieved through Dharma. All these are inter-related and complimentary. Elaborating these concepts he said, 'We have set the aim of developing body, mind, intellect as well as soul in a balanced way. We have tried to satisfy the manifold aspirations of man taking care that efforts to satisfy two different aspirations are not mutually conflicting. This is the integrated picture of all the fourfold aspirations of an individual. This concept of a complete human being, integral individual, is both our goal as well as our path.'[90]

---

[88]Ibid.
[89]Ibid.
[90]Ibid.

Lecture III: 24 April 1965

On the third day, he dwelt at length on various conceptual questions pertaining to the formation of society, role of individual, concept of nation as an organic entity and many others. He specifically dealt with the question as to how an individual stands vis-à-vis society, and whether society is in reality a result of 'Social Contract Theory' as espoused in the West. While raising the question whether 'society is a group of individuals brought into being by the individuals by an agreement among themselves',[91] he further wondered, 'If the individual produced a society then in whom the residual power remains vested, in the society or in the individual? Does the individual have the right to change the society? Can the society impose a variety or regulations on the individual and claim a right to the allegiance of the individual to itself? Or the individual is free as regards these questions?'[92] While rejecting the theory that society came into being as a result of a contract between individuals, he said that although society is composed of individuals, it's not formed by merely coming together of the individuals. He explained:

> In our view society is self-born. Like an individual, society comes into existence in an organic way. People do not produce society. It is not a sort of club, or some joint stock company, or a registered co-operative society. In reality, society is an entity with its own 'SELF', its own life; it is a sovereign being like an individual; it is an organic entity. We have not accepted the view that society is some arbitrary association. It has its own life. Society too has its body, mind, intellect and soul. Some Western psychologists are beginning to accept this truth.[93]

He further differed from the conceptualization that society and

[91]Ibid., http://deendayalupadhyay.org/leacture3.html
[92]Ibid.
[93]Ibid.

individuals are necessarily in conflict and that the society derived its dynamism from such a conflict. He saw conflict as detrimental to the progress of society and a sign of decadence and perversion. He said:

> We do not accept the view that there is any permanent inevitable conflict among the multifarious personality of an individual, and different institutions of the society. If a conflict does exist, it is a sign of decadence, perversion and not of nature or culture. The error in Western thinking lies in that some people there believe that human progress is a result of this fundamental conflict. Therefore they consider the conflict between the individual and the state as a natural occurrence; on the same basis they also theorized on the class conflict.[94]

Deendayal was of the opinion that Indian traditions focused on integration, cohesion and harmony. He accepted that classes existed in every society, but society should be seen as an organic whole; if the different parts of society are seen in conflict, then it cannot function properly. According to him, various institutions of the society may undergo deterioration due to a variety of reasons and sometimes, if the soul of the society is weakened, it affects its various limbs. He believed that family, community, trade union, gram panchayat, janapada, state and such other institutions are various limbs of the nation and even of mankind. They are interdependent, initially complementary. There should be a sense of unity through all of them. For this very reason, there should be a tendency towards mutual accommodation in them instead of conflict or opposition. While he emphasized the complementarities and interdependence of different institutions existing in harmony, he felt that the problem arises from the understanding wherein state is considered supreme. He said, 'State is one of the several

---

[94]Ibid.

institutions, an important one, but it is not above all other. One of the major reasons for the problems of the present-day world is that almost everyone thinks of the state to be synonymous with the society. At least in practice they consider the state as the sole representative of the society. Other institutions have declined in their effectiveness while the state has become dominant to such an extent that all the powers are gradually being centralized in the state.'[95] He further pointed out that in Indian understanding, state had a limited role and it was not above society. He substantiated it in the following words:

> We had not considered the state to be the sole representative of the nation. Our national life continued uninterruptedly even after the state went in the hands of foreigners. The Persian nation came to an end with their loss of independence. In our country, there were foreign rules now and then in various parts of the country. At some time the Pathans seized the throne of Delhi, and then the Turks; the Mughals and the British too established their rules. Despite all this, our national life went on, because the state was not its centre.[96]

But this too had its own share of problems. He quoted Dr B.R. Ambedkar who said that too strong gram panchayats led to neglect of the throne of Delhi. Such an approach led to weakening of the state as national life was not considered to be dependent on it. He said that although the state is not supreme, yet it is a very important institution. He further elaborated his point by citing the story of Samartha Guru Ramdas and Shivaji:

> Shri Ramdas would as well have preached to Shivaji to become a mendicant and spread Dharma following his own example. But on the contrary, he inspired Shivaji to extend his rule,

---

[95]Ibid.
[96]Ibid.

because state too, is an important institution of the society.[97]

Deendayal said that only by living together as a group on a piece of land does not constitute a nation. He said that there were examples of some ancient nations that perished even when the people were living together, 'The ancient Greek nation came to an end. Egyptian civilization, similarly, disappeared. Babylonian and Syrian civilizations are a matter of history. Was there ever a time when the citizens of those nations stopped living together?'[98] While on the other hand he says, 'Israeli Jews lived for centuries with other people, scattered far and wide, yet they did not get annihilated in the societies in which they lived because of cohabitation. It is clear therefore that the source of national feeling is not in staying on a particular piece of land, but is in something more.'[99] While defining a nation he said, 'When a group of persons live with a goal, an ideal, a mission, and looks upon a particular piece of land as motherland, this group constitutes a nation. If either of the two—an ideal and a motherland—is not there, then there is no nation.' He further said 'there is a "Self" in the body, the essence of the individual; upon the severance of its relation with the body, a person is said to die. Similarly there is this idea, ideal, or fundamental principle of a nation, its soul.'[100]

He further developed the concept of Chiti (soul of the nation), culture and Dharma as essential elements of a nation. He said, 'A human being is born with a soul. Human personality, soul and character are all distinct from one another. Personality results from a cumulative effect of all the actions, thoughts and impressions of an individual. But the soul is unaffected by this history. Similarly, national culture is continuously modified and enlarged by the

---

[97]Ibid.
[98]Ibid.
[99]Ibid.
[100]Ibid.

historic reasons and circumstances. Culture does include all those things which by the association, endeavours and the history of the society, have come to be held up as good and commendable but these are not added on to Chiti. Chiti is fundamental and is central to the nation from its very beginning. Chiti determines the direction in which the nation is to advance culturally. Whatever is in accordance with Chiti, is included in culture.'[101]

He further elaborated, 'If there is any standard for determining the merits and demerits of a particular action, it is this Chiti; from nature whatever is in accordance with Chiti, is approved and added on to culture. These things are to be cultivated. Whatever is against Chiti, is discarded as perversion, undesirable, is to be avoided. Chiti is the touchstone on which each action, each attitude is tested, and determined to be acceptable or otherwise. On the strength of this Chiti, a nation arises, strong and virile if it is this Chiti that is demonstrated in the actions of every great man of a nation.'[102]

He enriched the concept of nation with Dharma. For him Dharma was not religion but 'the laws that help manifest and maintain Chiti of a nation are termed Dharma of that nation. Hence it is this "Dharma" that is supreme. Dharma is the repository of the nation's soul. If Dharma is destroyed, the nation perishes. Anyone who abandons Dharma betrays the nation.'[103] Dharma is not a narrow concept as religion but it is very wider in meaning, it is one that covers all aspects of life, which sustains the society, nation and even the world. Dharma is supreme and even kings and gods abide by it and act as its protector. Dharma represents natural laws and even sustains the universe. He also talked about the concept of Dharma Rajya which is not a theocratic state, as Dharma and religion are different. In reality, a Dharma Rajya is a state in which all the religions have freedom to practise their own religion. In a

---

[101]Ibid.
[102]Ibid.
[103] Ibid.

Dharma Rajya, state is not sovereign, but subject to Dharma, and sovereignty is actually vested in Dharma. It is also not about the majority rule but rule of Dharma. While giving several examples to clarify the argument he said, 'Let us understand very clearly that Dharma is not necessarily with the majority or with the people. Dharma is eternal. Therefore, in the definition of democracy to say that it is a government of the people, is not enough, it has to be for the good of the people. What constitutes the good of the people Dharma alone can decide. Therefore, a democratic Government, Jana Rajya, must also be rooted in Dharma i.e. a Dharma Rajya. In the definition of 'Democracy' viz. 'government of the people, by the people and for the people', 'of' stands for independence, 'by' stands for democracy and 'for' indicates Dharma. Therefore, the true democracy is only where there is freedom as well as Dharma encompasses all these concepts.'[104]

Lecture IV: 25 April 1965

He delivered his fourth and final lecture on 25 April 1965. While he delved at length on the functions of state and nation in his third lecture, elaborating on the organic nature of nation as per Bharatiya traction, he focused on the various aspects of economy in his final lecture. He discussed the manner in which Western economics, whether capitalist or socialist, had inhuman and unethical approach as it gave 'value' a central position in its scheme of things. He said the slogan of 'one must earn his bread' should be replaced by 'the one who earns will feed and every person will have enough to eat... The right to food is a birthright. The ability to earn is a result of education and training. In a society, even those who do not earn must have food. The children and the old, the diseased and the invalids, all must be cared for by the society.'[105] While elaborating

---

[104]Ibid, http://deendayalupadhyay.org/leacture11.html

[105]Ibid, http://deendayalupadhyay.org/leacture4.html

this argument he said that a man works not for bread alone but to fulfil his other responsibilities in the society. He further added, 'Any economic system must provide for the minimum basic necessities of human life to everyone. Food, clothing and shelter constitute, broadly speaking, these basic necessities. Similarly, the society must enable the individual to carry out his obligations to the society by properly educating him. Lastly, in the event of an individual falling prey to any disease, society must arrange for his treatment and maintenance. If a government provides these minimum requirements, only then it is a rule of Dharma. Otherwise, it is a rule of Adharma.'[106]

He considered education a social responsibility as it helped the society in achieving its goals in the long run. While citing the example that no fees were charged by the princely states and higher education, along with boarding and lodging, was provided for free in the gurukulas of ancient India, he said, 'To educate a child is in the interest of the society itself. By birth a child is an animal. He becomes a responsible member of the society only by education and culture. To charge fees for something which is in the interest of the society itself is rather odd. If due to the inability to pay the fees, children are left without education, will the society endure the situation for long? We do not charge fee from trees for sowing the seed and caring for the supplying. On the contrary we invest our money and efforts. We know that when the tree grows, we shall reap fruits.'[107]

One of the main concerns of Deendayal was to ensure guarantee of work to every individual. An individual not participating in the production activities may become a liability to the society, and if individual participation is obstructed, the system becomes self-destructive. Since man has stomach and hands, his natural progress

---

[106]Ibid.
[107]Ibid.

requires them to work, otherwise there will be distortion and lop-sided growth. He said, 'The guarantee of work to every able-bodied member of the society should be the aim of our economic system. Today we witness a very strange situation. On the one hand, a ten-year-old child and a seventy-year-old man are toiling and on the other hand a youth of twenty-five is driven to suicide for want of work. We shall have to remove this mismanagement. God has given hands to every man, but by themselves hands have a limited capacity to produce. They need assistance of capital in the form of machines. Labour and capital bear the same relation to each other as that between man and nature. The world is a creation of these two. Neither of them can be neglected.'[108]

While speaking on why capital formation can be suitably done in Indian environment, he supported the idea of restrain on consumption and decentralization of economy. He said, 'In the capitalist system the industrialist creates capital with the help of this surplus value. In a socialist system, the state undertakes this task. In both the systems, the entire production is not distributed among the workers. If production is carried on through centralized large-scale industries, the sacrifice on the part of the worker in creating the capital is not given due recognition. The advantage in decentralization is in the fact that the workers have a sense of direct participation in the management of this surplus value or capital.'[109] He further said machines were created to enhance the productivity of the worker and not as his competitor. He said that the real problem started when the worker was considered a commodity and machine was seen as his competitor. The Western world faced the crisis of the worker, so they designed their machines accordingly. But in India circumstances were different, and so we needed to develop our own machines and tools. He emphasized

---

[108]Ibid.
[109]Ibid.

Prof. Vishvesaraya's seven 'M's, viz. man, material, money, management, motive power, market and machine in production process. He was in favour of the system in which every worker found a job. He said that like it was a loss when a part of factory remained unutilized, similarly it was also a loss for the nation if a part of its workforce was rendered jobless. He further said, 'Therefore instead of the usual exhortation "Every worker must get food", we must think of "Everyone who eats must get work", as the basis of our economy. No doubt charakha has to be replaced by machines, but not necessarily automatic machines everywhere. Full employment must be a primary consideration and then the rest of the six factors suit this.'[110]

Deendayal also discussed the question of 'Man's place in the Economy' and said, 'The use of manpower and the employment question will have to be thought of in the context of the human being as a whole, as an integral being. The economic theories of the past few centuries and the structure of society based on these theories, have resulted in a thorough devaluation of the human being. His personality is altogether irrelevant to the economic set up.'[111] He said that capitalist economy saw worker as 'economic man' and as a commodity to be purchased and sold in a system in which elimination of the weak was considered natural and justified. Such a worker was considered uneconomic, marginal unit, not fit to exist. As far as socialist economy was concerned, it had emerged as a reaction to capitalism and only believed in transferring ownership of capital to state without recognizing the importance of a human being. As state was an impersonal being operating on rigid manual of rules and regulations, it failed to recognize the individuality and individual discretion of a worker. While evaluating the situation, he wrote, 'The capitalistic system thought merely of the economic

---

[110]Ibid, http://deendayalupadhyay.org/leacture12.html
[111]Ibid.

man, but left him free in other fields where he could exercise his individuality. The socialist system went much further thinking only of the abstract man. After that, there was no scope for the development of the individual personality based on diverse tastes and abilities. The needs and preferences of individuals have as much importance in the socialist system as in a prison manual. There is no such thing as individual freedom in the socialist system.'[112]

While rooting for an 'Integral Man', Deendayal supported 'Decentralization' and 'Swadeshi'. He said, 'Both these systems, capitalist as well as communist, have failed to take account of the Integral Man, his true and complete personality and his aspirations. One considers him a mere selfish being lingering after money, having only one law, the law of fierce competition, in essence the law of the jungle; whereas the other has viewed him as a feeble lifeless cog in the whole scheme of things, regulated by rigid rules, and incapable of any good unless directed. The centralization of power, economic and political, is implied in both. Both, therefore, result in dehumanization of man.'[113] Man being the highest creation of God, he believed, needed to be re-established to his rightful position. He suggested the following objectives of economy:

- An assurance of minimum standard of living to every individual and preparedness for the defense of the nation.
- Further increase above this minimum standard of living whereby the individual and the nation acquire the means to contribute to the world progress on the basis of its own Chiti.
- To provide means of employment to every able-bodied citizens by which the above two objectives can be realized, and to avoid waste and extravagance in utilizing

---

[112]Ibid.

[113]Deendayal Sansar: A complete Deendayal Reader, *Cultural Basis of Independence*, Selected Thoughts, http://deendayalupadhyay.org/culture.htmlreference

natural resources.

- To develop suitable machines for Bharatiya conditions (Bharatiya Technology) taking note of the availability and nature of the various factors of production (seven 'M's).
- This system must help and not disregard the human being, the individual. It must protect the cultural and other values of life. This is a requirement which cannot be violated except at a risk of great peril.
- The ownership—state, private or any other form—of industries must be decided on a pragmatic and practical basis.

Based on the above directions, he said that the economy could be moved on the path of decentralization and swadeshi. He rued the fact that the planners had become prisoners of the thought that large scale and centralized industries were the only way out for Indian economy to grow. Similarly, 'swadeshi' was ridiculed as old fashioned and reactionary, and 'we have grown over-independent on foreign aid...from thinking, management, capital, methods of production, technology, etc. to even the standards and forms of consumption. He felt that such an approach would make India a slave of others and the need of the hour was to use 'swadeshi' as an important component in the programme of national reconstruction.

EVALUATING HIS IDEAS AND PHILOSOPHY

As the leadership of independent India attempted to find solutions to its various problems by finding ways through Western political ideas of secularism, individualism, communism and its various other 'isms', Deendayal doubted the efficacy of such an approach. He raised the question that when the Western imperialism stood rejected, how such 'isms' might prove useful in the long run for a country like India. Almost all the established parties understood that these 'isms' would have to be accepted with some amendments, because we lacked any alternative political thought. They believed that it was the Britishers, who on coming to India, created a nation, and after they left, India became a 'nation in the making'. On the other hand, Deendayal considered India as an ancient and eternal nation, and the idea of India's 'cultural nationalism' much older than the Western idea of 'nation-state'. He felt that the path towards India's future might be paved by its glorious knowledge of traditions which had a comprehensive and integrated vision.

He further believed that the Western vision of looking at man was divided; its individualism was the enemy of socialism and socialism was the enemy of individualism. They wanted victory of man over nature; nature versus man became their equation. By adopting secularism they snapped spiritualism from the public life, therefore dialectical equations of materialism versus spiritualism, state versus church and religion versus science emerged. He believed that this debate of the West was also a human debate; we should know about it and learn from it but we should not become a follower of dialectical conclusions. The Indian idea led to an integral approach and did not bank itself on piecemeal approach like the West, which talked in terms of 'individual versus society', 'man versus nature', etc. Never did it talk in terms of integration, cohesion and harmony between individual and society or between man and nature. It assumed a thread of integration and harmony in the apparent separateness. Such an approach resulted in man considering himself an individual, and everyone else his enemy. That led him to wage war against social institutions, family, caste, kinship, panchayat, etc. In the name of socialism he was creating dictatorship, in the name of development he was fighting against nature, he was inviting destructions by destroying the environment. By rejecting spiritualism he had become the slave of his senses. He was only earning sorrow in his search for happiness and had become unaware of the concept of happiness.

Deendayal said that Indian tradition rejects this separateness and establishes its relationship with both the unconscious and conscious. Earth is mother, moon is maternal uncle (mama), mountain is god, and river is mother. The ideas of Integral Humanism believes that every individual of the society is mutually linked, this world is not an alien place, this earth is family, and that there is a need to free everyone from the ideas of separateness, alienation and dialectical relationship. Integration is present in completeness. In the lack of completeness, man is affected by partial vision. As the universe is complete, so is an individual. The individual does not only mean his physical being; he has a mind, an intellect and a soul. If any one of these four is ignored, the happiness of man will be handicapped; he needs integral and intense happiness, called joy or bliss. In the same manner, society does not only consist of a government; it has its own culture, people and country. Without the proper movement of these four, happiness is not possible. The man integrated with vyashti, samashti, srishti and parameshthi is virat. Its goals (purusharth) are four dimensional. Dharma, artha, kama, moksha are situation-neutral goals, and the society and its system's work is to fulfil them.

Dharma: Means education, culture and legal system

Artha: Means sadhan purusharth ('means') that includes economy, employment, production, distribution, utility, etc. as per Dharma.

Kama 'Dharmavirudh Kamoaham': Means all indulgences come true. One has to make them positive by giving them cultural moderation through music and different arts. Kama in opposition to Dharma is not purushartha, but distortion.

Moksha: Means the highest goal and is achieved when an individual is free from the complexities of scarcity and influence.

The main ideas of Pandit Deendayal Upadhyaya may be seen in his conceptualization of Bharatiyata, Dharma, Dharmarajya and Antyodaya. By Bharatiyata he meant Bharatiya culture which, unlike Western thoughts, saw life as an integrated whole. Bharatiyata, according to him, could manifest itself not through politics but through culture. If India had anything to offer to the world, then it was the feeling of cultural tolerance and a life dedicated to duty. He further said, 'From the national standpoint we shall have to consider our culture because that is our very nature. Independence is intimately related to one's own culture. If culture does not form the basis of independence, then the political movement for independence would degenerate into a scramble by selfish and power-seeking persons. Independence can be meaningful only if it becomes an instrument for the expression of our culture. Such expression will not only contribute to our progress but the effort required will also give us the experience of joy.'[114]

He was completely opposed to the attempts to equate Dharma with religion. Religion, a mode of worship, has a very limited meaning but Dharma stands for a wide term, including many religions. According to him, religion meant a creed, or a sect, it did not mean Dharma. Being a very broad concept, Dharma is concerned with all aspects of life. It sustains society. It sustains the whole world. That which sustains is Dharma. The fundamental principles of Dharma are eternal and universal. Yet their implementation may differ according to time, place and circumstances. The complete treatise on the rules in general and their philosophical basis is the meaning of Dharma.

While describing Dharmarajya, he considered state to be one of the constituent within the nation, and not above it. In theorizing thus, he never intended to undermine the importance of state in the society or democracy but attempted to emphasize the pluralistic

---

[114]Deendayal Sansar: A complete Deendayal Reader, *Cultural Basis of Independence*, Selected Thoughts, http://deendayalupadhyay.org/culture.htmlreference

character of the society and the nation. He gave a very interesting explanation as to why a Jana Rajya (democratic state) should also be a Dharmarajya. He said, 'Let us understand very clearly that Dharma is not necessarily with the majority or with the people. Dharma is eternal. Therefore, in the definition of democracy, to say that it is a government of the people is not enough; it has to be for the good of the people. Dharma alone can decide. Therefore, a democratic government, "Jana Rajya", must also be rooted in Dharma i.e. a "Dharma Rajya". In the definition of "Democracy" viz. "government of the people, by the people and for the people", "of" stands for independence, "by" stands for democracy, and "for" indicates Dharma. Therefore the true democracy is one where there is freedom as well as Dharma.'[115] His concept of Dharmarajya can be understood more elaborately from the following attributes, which form the fundamental principles based on which a ruler should act:

1. The ruler is the upholder of Dharma, not its creator. Nor can he decide as to what Dharma is. He is responsible only for its proper enforcement. Dharma means those eternal and universal laws which are conducive to the sustenance of our life and the universe—those laws which our rishis have discovered through their prescience. On a small scale, they reflect in the most distinctive and fundamental characteristics of the way of life of a nation, on the maintenance of which depends the very persistence of a particular nation. In short, Dharma is the life process of a nation, and marks itself out from other nations. It is the sacred duty of the ruler to protect this life process, i.e. Dharma.

2. Dharmarajya is also inclusive of Gandhiji's Ram Rajya when he defines a ruler as Raja iti Ranjati. That is, a ruler

---

[115]Deendayal Sansar: A complete Deendayal Reader, Dharma and Religion, Selected Thoughts, http://deendayalupadhyay.org/drama.html

cannot claim to be a ruler in the true sense of the term unless he works for the welfare of all.[116]

Antyodaya, although a word belonging to Gandhian lexicon, was built on the ideas of Pandit Deendayal Upadhyaya. His vision of 'education for all' and 'har hath ko kam, har khet ko pani' was seen culminating in his idea of Economic Democracy. Explaining his idea of Economic Democracy, he said, 'If a vote for everyone is the touchstone of political democracy, work for everyone is a measure of economic democracy. This right to work does not mean slave labour as in communist countries. Work should not only give a means of livelihood to a person but it should be of the choice of that person. If for doing that work the worker does not get a proper share in the national income, he would be considered unemployed. From this point of view a minimum wage, a just system of distribution and some sort of social security are necessary.'[117] Opposing the ideas of large scale industries based development, centralization and monopoly, he advocated swadeshi and decentralization. He further said that any system which reduced the opportunity for employment was undemocratic. He advocated a system free from social inequality where the capital and power got decentralized. As a staunch opponent of both capitalism and communism, he felt that the path for India was through encouraging the sectors of self employment for which a system was required, wherein maximum production could be done by employing maximum hands. He was an ardent supporter of an integral village which could be self-sufficient and self-reliant. He had a vision of increased production, restraint consumption and equitable distribution. He

---

[116]Parmeshwaran, P (Ed.), *Gandhi, Lohia and Deendayal*, Deendayal Research Institute, New Delhi, 1978, p. 40

[117]Deendayal Sansar: A complete Deendayal Reader, *Economic Democracy, Dharma and religion*, Selected Thoughts, http://deendayalupadhyay.org/economics.html

was also opposed to unrestrained exploitation of nature and felt that the nature should be used as per our need, and not for people's greed. Pandit Deendayal Upadhyaya's messages to the world are:

1. Building a strong and prosperous Indian nation on the foundation of Indian culture
2. Dharmarajya (which guartantees freedom, equality and justice to all)
3. Sarvodaya and Antyodaya (maximum good to all)
4. Samanvaya (synthesis, not conflict, as the basis of life)[118]

As we evaluate the contribution of Deendayal, a great thinker and leader, the need of the hour is to follow his ideas and principles which are aimed at making politics a tool for service to the nation. He stood rock solid defending Indian civilizational values and culture in the time when the Western ideas were ruling the world, and many great thinkers, philosophers and leaders of that time were swept away by its torrential current. He not only stood his ground but defined Indian ethos and value system in the context of changing time and the need of the hour. Today, we can say that he was as much right in his assertions as he was firm in his convictions. While the Marxist and capitalist ideologies have created havoc in the world, his ideas, attuned to the Indian civilizational values, show us the path to be followed in the future.

---

[118]Parmeshwaran, P (Ed.), *Gandhi, Lohia and Deendayal*, Deendayal Research Institute, New Delhi, 1978, p. 46.

MESSAGE OF HIS LIFE

If one has to describe Deendayalji, then his entire personality has to be seen in four parts. First, he was a thinker and ideologue who presented original ideas. Second, he was an all-round organizer who embraced the path of harmony in a political environment full of doubts and contradictions. Third, he was also a hard-working and ideal leader. Lastly, he was an untiring explorer making a new path in politics through boundless patience, self confidence and devotion, inspiring people to tread on the new path and having courage to do so himself.[119]

—Amit Shah

As a political figure and an ideologue, Deendayal continues to inspire political activists across ideological spectrum and, more particularly, those belonging to BJP. He serves as a role model for aspiring youth and is considered a conscience keeper of the leadership and activists. BJP leaders, including some of the top leaders of other parties, refer to him as an example in their political discourses to be emulated as he stands out from the rest of his contemporaries, owing to his intellectual abilities and political

---

[119]Presidential address on the occasion of Pt Deendayal Upadhyaya centenary celebrations in Kozhikode, Kerela on 25 September 2016, Adhyakshiya Bhashan, Rashtriya Parishad Baithak, Bharatiya Janata Party, 2016

acumen. His main contribution lies in defining political ideology and heralding an era of coalition governments in pursuance of creating alternative for Congress and its politics. He also tried to present an ideal picture of a political activist, the 'Karyakarta', through his conduct in public life. An ideologue, a political leader, an activist, an organizer, all combined in one, Deendayal is still represented as an ideal swayamsevak, and as an icon for the party activists and leaders. His high intellect, grasp over organizational skills, political understanding and indomitable spirit remained covered under his simplicity and a very ordinary lifestyle. Bhaurao Deoras, who was prant-pracharak (RSS head) of Uttar Pradesh when Deendayal was sah-prantpracharak (Bhaurao Deodas's deputy), praised Deendayal for being a constant source of inspiration for the Sangh.

Deendayal was a highly motivated swayamsevak who chose to embark on a lifelong journey of untiring work and unflinching ideological commitments. His letter to his maternal uncle on 21 July 1942, that showed his eagerness to commit himself as a lifelong pracharak of RSS, gave an insight into his resolve to become part of a movement in which he saw the solutions to the problems faced by the nation. It was not wrong for his family to expect him to settle down after completing his education, but Deendayal's destiny had planned something very different for him. It was not that he wasn't aware of his maternal uncle's expectations, who brought him up as his son, but the call of duty to a larger cause made him commit his life to RSS and its mission. The dilemma which he considered 'a fierce battle' between 'sentiments and obligations' pulled him in different directions. He seemed to have resolved it too, as he explained himself to his uncle in a letter that said 'Duty shall ever triumph over sentiment'. The manner in which he pleaded with his uncle gave a glimpse of his resolve to dedicate himself to larger goals. He wrote:

'God has blessed our family with everything. Can we not then offer at least one of our members for the service of the country? Having provided me with education, moral instructions and all sorts of qualifications, can you not now give me back to the samaj to which we owe so much? This will hardly be any kind of sacrifice, it will rather be an investment... Can we not forgo few worthless ambitions for the protection and benefit of a samaj and a faith for which Rama suffered exile, Krishna bore innumerable hardships, Rana Pratap roamed about from forest to forest, Shivaji staked his all and Guru Gobind Singh allowed his little sons to be buried alive?'[120]

As he came in contact with Sangh, Deendayal tried to live the principles which were central to the organizational ethos of RSS. As Sangh encouraged a swayamsevak to work with self inspiration and self discipline, he inculcated these qualities in his personality and set himself as an example for the party karyakartas. Guruji Gowalkar in his condolence speech in Jaunpur remembered Deendayal's contribution in glowing terms. He said, 'He occupied the foremost place among those few who realize their duty as swayamsevaks of the Sangh very early in life, and devote their total energies and dedicate their life to the mission of the Sangh. It is expected of a Sangh swayamsevak that he should develop and keep active all the qualities of a swayamsevak and remain loyal to the organization; that he should bear in mind the importance of all activities of the Sangh and participate in them; and that he should successfully carry out whatever duties he is asked to perform and in whatever field, as did Deendayalji, who was allocated work in the field of politics. It should not be an exaggeration to say that what is Jana Sangh today is his creation, that its stature in the country is the fruit of his unremitting efforts. To him alone goes the credit of starting from scratch and building up such an imposing organization from its very foundation.'[121]

---

[120]Sharma, Mahesh Chandra, *Deendayal Upadhyaya: Sampoorna Vangmaya*, vol. I, Prabhat Prakashan, 2016.

[121]http://www.kamalsandesh.org/ideal-swayamsevak/

HIS SIMPLICITY

The foundation of an organization is not only laid in theories, but also in the manner in which its leadership practises those theories in life. Deendayal presented an example to his party activists by practising a very simple life. It was his simplicity that inculcated a culture of selfless service as one of the cardinal principles of the organization. It not only enabled him to connect to the party activists, but also strengthen their resolve in the high principles on which Jana Sangh was formed. He represented an ordinary karyakarta with an extraordinary capacity which was unique and even matchless. For him organizational hierarchy was only a system, and in reality all were karyakartas. Unlike the popular image of political leaders donning the mantle of erstwhile feudal lords, rajas and maharajas, he symbolized a very simple man in ordinary attires. K.R. Malkani wrote about his first impression about Deendayal:

'I must say I was not particularly impressed when I first saw him during period of the ban on RSS way back in 1948. But I found that the bright young swayamsevaks of UP already treated him with reverence. They were right. For years I called him "Deendayal". But as I saw more and more of him, I, too unconsciously switched over to "Panditji". It was a quiet tribute to the quality of the man and his leadership.'[122]

Deendayal was initiated into activism through Sangh and he deeply imbibed the qualities expected of a swayamsevak and a pracharak. As he dedicated himself as a lifelong pracharak of Sangh, all these qualities manifested in his personality, enabling him to expand Sangh's work—earlier as sah-prantpracharak and later in Jana Sangh as its general secretary and president. Satyavrat Sinha wrote, 'He was indeed the most representative product of Sangh. He embodied in himself such fine qualities as modesty, dedication,

---

[122]Raje, Sudhakar (Ed.), *Pt. Deendayal Upadhyaya: A Profile*, Deendayal Research Institute, New Delhi, 1992, p. 80.

genuine indifference to publicity, resolute courage, organizing skill, love for the people and cooperative spirit, deep thinking, discipline and self control.'[123] All these qualities seemed difficult to practise, but Deendayal experimented with these in the political arena and was able to build a network of dedicated karyakartas who laid the strong foundation of Jana Sangh. It could be said that these qualities, which were rare in politics, made it possible for Jana Sangh to nurture a culture of selfless service, commitment to ideology and larger goals in the organization.

He never saw politics as a tool for aggrandizement of power, but a mission for regeneration of national life. According to his longtime associate and former Prime Minister Atal Bihari Vajpayee, 'Politics was the means and not the end in itself. It was the way to his destination, not the destination itself. He was never fascinated by any post. He was not a member of parliament himself; rather he was the maker of parliamentarians. He never hankered after office. It was after great persuasion that he could be made to accept the office of President of the Party.'[124]

L.K. Advani was a longtime associate of Deendayal and worked closely with him. On 25 September 1977, on the occasion of Deendayal's birthday celebration, he delivered a speech as minister of Information and Broadcasting in Janata Party government. This speech was later published under the title 'My Simple Hero':

According to a saying in English, 'No man is a hero of his valet.' This means no man is great to those who are closest to him, for they have the opportunity to observe him at very close quarters and gets to know his shortcomings. Rather, it happens many times that when you go very close to a great man, he seems small. But what has been the experience

---

[123]Ibid, p. 68.
[124]Jha, Prabhat, *The Ajaatshatru Deendayalji*, Dr. Mookerjee Smruti Nyas, New Delhi, 2011, p. 5.

of those of us who came in contact with Pandit Deendayal Upadhyaya? It was my great fortune that after entering the political field I could all the time receive his guidance as long as he was alive. And the more I think of him the more I feel his greatness.[125]

Dr Murli Manohar Joshi who had the opportunity to work with Deendayal in his young days wrote:

On one occasion, a karyakarta was deputed to take Deendayalji by his motor car to the venue where a meeting was scheduled. The motor car broke down and it could not reach the station. I owned a motorcycle those days. Without any hesitation he took a ride on my motorcycle to reach the venue on time. There he addressed a predominantly rural gathering. It was a pleasant surprise to see him discussing the hardships faced by rural people. Needless to say, he could easily strike a chord with the ordinary farmers living in villages. Most of the time he never informed us about his arrival in advance. I had seen him coming to my house even in a rickshaw.[126]

Vachnesh Tripathi recounted one incident which showed how Deendayal used to lead by setting an example among his co-workers. He wrote:

A chronic shortage of funds sometimes led to the shortage of workers in the 'Panchjanaya' office. The few who were employed were complaining; they found it difficult to keep up with time-schedule of the work, which is essential of a journal. Upadhyayaji understood the problem, and silently heard everyone's complaint. He started on a pile of bill to

[125]Advani, L.K., 'My Simple Hero', *Destination*, Deendayal Research Institute, New Delhi, 1978, p. 38.
[126]Jha, Prabhat, *The Ajaatshatru Deendayalji*, Dr. Mookerjee Smruti Nyas, New Delhi, 2011, p. 12.

be written. In an hour or two he finished it and the example of his devotion inspired others too. The work of printing and dispatching which seemed so formidable at first, was tackled with zeal.

Panditji had written all the bills, but it was not in his nature to seek rest. He volunteered to take the bundle to the station. A bicycle was borrowed for him—the Managing Director of Rashtra Dharma Prakashan. We reached the station in time and he saw to it that the packages and bundles were properly posted when the mail train arrived.[127]

One incident, as told by Shiv Kumar Asthana, showed how his simplicity was also rooted in his innocence. Asthana wrote:

In August 1961 a reception was arranged in honour of Deendayalji by the Chandousi College Union. After welcoming him at the station we took him to the residence of District Sangh Secretary Shri Manoharlal. That day he was dressed in an extraordinary manner—a soiled shirt of cheap, ordinary cloth, a threadbare dhoti with patches all over, and a cotton pair of shoes with holes through which a toe was peeping out. But he seemed the least worried about it. Before leaving for the college, Shri Manoharlal brought a dhoti, a shirt and a pair of shoes, and requested him to change into them. Panditji smiled and said very simply, 'Why, I have just toured all over UP but nobody seemed to mind. Has Chandousi become so big?' We were at a loss to reply. But somehow we managed to get him to change.

The programme at the college was very impressive. On returning home Shri Manoharlal went inside to make arrangements for tea and refreshments. A shock awaited

---

[127]Raje, Sudhakar (Ed.), *Pt. Deendayal Upadhyaya: A Profile*, Deendayal Research Institute, New Delhi, 1992, p. 96.

him on return—he found that Panditji had removed the new clothes, folded them up and had got back into his old clothes.

We were caught dumbfounded in an awkward position; Shri Manoharlal pleaded with folded hands, 'Panditji, why are you putting us to shame? Why did you remove the clothes?'

Panditji smiled and asked, 'You mean you had given them to me?' All present were charmed by his innocence. With great difficulty could we manage him to change again.[128]

Balram Das Tandon said, 'In the early 1960s, once we all karyakartas were waiting for him at Amritsar railway station but the train was running late. Thus, all karyakartas returned to the Sangh office, except for me and a few others who stayed on to inquire about the exact timing of the train's arrival so that arrangements to receive him were accordingly rescheduled. In the meantime, the station master came and informed us that the train would arrive at Amritsar station around 5.00 p.m. We waited in the Jana Sangh office till 4.00 p.m. and were about to leave for the railway station to receive him when at 4.30 p.m., we saw Shri Deendyalji enter the office holding his briefcase and carrying a small bundle of bedding in his hands. He acknowledged the greetings of everybody present there with a smile on his face. When we expressed our apologies for not being present at the platform to receive him at the station, smilingly he replied, 'A late-comer should be treated like that.'[129]

Many such incidents have been recounted, illustrating his deep faith in the dictum of simple living and high thinking. He rarely cared about his attires and looks, yet his personality had the magnetic appeal, making him a very unique individual of a rare genre. Once Deendayal was to visit the USA, and suitable clothes were arranged for the purpose. On his return, he gave those clothes

---

[128]Ibid, pp. 94–95.
[129]Jha, Prabhat, *The Ajaatshatru Deendayalji*, Dr. Mookerjee Smruti Nyas, New Delhi, 2011, pp. 170–171.

back, along with foreign currencies, to Jana Sangh Office Secretary Jagdish Mathur, saying that since all his needs, including board and lodging, were looked after by the party workers, he did not have to spend anything at all. He was a class apart in politics who believed in selfless service to the nation and was deeply committed to his principles. He was a saint in politics—simple, innocent and yet charming. He was neither tempted by glamour nor overtaken by power politics.

AN EXAMPLE IN POLITICS

Deendayal had a different notion of politics. It was a mission, a commitment and a medium to achieve goals envisaged by the sages, seers, martyrs and people of India. Atal Bihari Vajpayee wrote, 'He wanted to inject spiritualism in politics. He derived inspiration from the glorious past of India and wanted to make her future still more magnificent. His faith took inspiration from indestructible roots of ancient India but he was never a conservative. He started his journey of life with the sole objective in mind to make India a prosperous and modern nation.'[130]

He was an organizer par excellence. As an organizer, he valued the karyakartas and the collectivism which was required to be nurtured in a culture of oneness and unity. For this end, each individual was to constitute a whole. He preferred to submerge his individuality in the collective whole to build a strong foundation of the organization. L.K. Advani narrated an incident which showed how Deendayal preferred to use 'We' instead of 'I'. He wrote, 'For some time, Deendayalji did send the article mentioning about his experiences during the tour. Later, he stopped writing. One day I went to him and said that we were not receiving his article these days. He said, Lal, "I will not be able to write it any more." I could

---

[130]Ibid, p. 5.

very well understand the reason for his not doing so. For writing such a piece, he had to mention about himself in the article and he did not wish to project himself in his writings. Doing so he had to use the word "I" a number of times and that is what he despised all along. He did not wish to devote his time in thinking and writing about himself.'[131]

While narrating an incident about how Deendayal cared for karyakartas and left an indelible mark on him, Dr Murli Manohar Joshi wrote, 'I came in contact with Deendayalji in 1949. That was the time when a ban had been imposed on the RSS. He was the sah-prantpracharak in Uttar Pradesh. We invited him to give a lecture at my college. Students from socialist and communist parties worked overnight to make the proposed programme a big flop. Deendayalji came and the programme started on time. I, along with my friends, went out to ensure that no untoward incident should take place in the campus during Pandit Deendayal Upadhyaya's speech. Attempting to disrupt the programme, a group of students removed the electric fuse. We immediately rushed to make other alternatives for light. It was done in such a great hurry that I fell down and got hurt. In spite of their best efforts, the students from Communist wings could not succeed in their nefarious design and the meeting ended in a success. We went back to our hostel rooms. When Deendayalji came to know about us being hurt, he came to see us in our hostel rooms. After that I remained in constant touch with him till he left for his heavenly abode.'[132]

He was not only known for his concern for the karyakartas, he never hesitated to defend them when they were in some kind of trouble or committed a mistake unintentionally. The story of Pandhari Rao Kridutta, an MLA in Madhya Pradesh assembly, was always cited as an example for his concern for karyakartas.

---

[131]Ibid, p. 08.
[132]Ibid, p. 10.

Kushabhau Thakre wrote about the story in following words:

> Pandhari Rao Kridutta had some heated arguments with the Speaker. There was a big furore in the Assembly. Amidst all this uproar, a shoe was thrown at the chair. Kriduttaji was blamed for it and suspended. We immediately called Deendayalji and told him the whole story. A meeting was convened. Deendayalji presided over the meeting and discussed the situation. Addressing the press later he said that one should not ignore the circumstances which precipitated such an extreme action. On being asked by journalists, Panditji said very calmly, 'You have seen Pandhari Raoji during the last 3–4 years in the assembly. Did he ever get angry that much in the past? If not, then what were the circumstances that made him so angry that day? Without going into the circumstances that led to this incident, it will not be right for me to comment. As far as the incident goes, it cannot be justified. But I would repeat that the conduct of those because of whom this situation arose must also be looked into.
>
> While leaving the meeting he again emphasized, 'Pandhari Rao, the nature of anger should always be genuine and virtuous.'
>
> After this incident another meeting was held at Ambala. Deendayalji had to present a detailed report as he was the general secretary. He did not mention the incident relating to Kriduttaji. The then Jana Sangh President Balraj Madhok was not pleased at this 'omission'. Deendayalji defended his decision and said that the party president should not expect him to behave like a policeman. He added, he could not discredit or demoralize any committed party worker. He always sympathized with the party cadre.[133]

---

[133]Ibid, pp. 22–23

Pandhari Rao Kridutta, while narrating the incident, said that Deendayal never demoralized committed partymen. He wrote, 'My resignation was also demanded by some people... But Panditji changed the whole scenario by saying that the incident should be reviewed as a whole and a decision taken afterwards. With these words he neither encouraged me nor did he discourage me. While leaving the meeting he again emphasized, "Pandhari Rao, the nature of anger should always be genuine and virtuous." I was overwhelmed by Deendayalji's reaction.'[134]

He never avoided anyone and was always available for his karyakartas. It was probably his exposure to the ground work in his life that he always valued the importance of the karyakartas and their emotional attachment to the organization. He loved to meet everyone and enjoyed personal relationship with a large number of karyakartas. While recounting an incident, Jagdish Prasad Mathur wrote, 'I recall an incident when we were staying at the very humble residence of a party worker in Dataganj, a small town in Badaun district of Uttar Pradesh. Someone came to see Deendayalji. Since I knew that the person was somewhat unbalanced, I asked him to leave. He did. When Deendayalji asked if someone had come to see him, I told him about that person. He upbraided me saying that the person might be mentally deranged, but he was a swayamsevak nevertheless. "What harm would have come if he had met me?" he asked.'[135]

He listened to everyone and tried to find solutions by giving minute attention to every aspect of the problem. Balram Das Tandon wrote, 'It was Upadhyayji's nature to patiently listen to everybody and satisfactorily respond to all queries made to him, whether these related to one's personal life, the party organisation or one's own organisation's internal problems. Even if somebody

---

[134]Ibid, p. 88.
[135]Ibid, p. 37.

asked for his guidance on some personal issues, he was too pleased to offer his views immediately.'[136]

It was his personal touch to the karyakartas and deep understanding about them that helped Deendayal to nurture the organization into a family. He enjoyed personal relationhips with the karykartas that developed a bonding which emotionally connected him with them and made him take proper care of·their organizational engagements. The organization was developed as a family on the firm foundation of mutual affection, respect and understanding. He also applied the concept of human organization where an unintentional mistake was tolerated, and attempts were made to be sensitive of each other's capacity and limitations. He always tried to inculcate mutual love, trust and confidence among the karyakartas, and moulded them into an effective team that worked for ideology and organization, rather than for their self interests. It was made possible by setting himself as an example and developing an organizational culture woven on the basis of commitment towards the larger goals.

INTERNAL DEMOCRACY

Deendayal always believed in internal democracy in the organization. The decision making in the organization were mostly on the basis of dialogue, discussions and meetings through which the issues were sorted out and consensus were built on various questions faced by the party. It not only helped in strengthening the organization, but created a team spirit and positive atmosphere for the acceptance of final decision. He also ensured that the karykartas had the sense of participation in the decision making of the party. He also modified his own opinions on the basis of the inputs received from others, and accepted the decision which appeared to him

---

[136]Ibid, p. 172.

as the natural outcome of the dialogues and discussions in the party meetings. Kushabhau Thakre said that Deendayal was not very keen in forming coalition government when Congress lost the elections. He wrote, 'In 1967, the Opposition parties outnumbered the Congress in Madhya Pradesh Assembly, as the Congress could win only 142 seats whereas the Opposition won 146 seats. But Deendayalji decided not to make any effort to form a coalition government because he was aware of the temperament of the socialists. He never approved of horse trading in politics. He always felt that "politics is not an easy way and it follows a slippery path. Only those survive who take to this path keeping larger interests of the people in mind."'[137]

But later Deendayal modified his decision on the basis of the outcome of the meeting which he held with newly-elected legislators. While saying that Deendayal always consulted local leadership, Kailash Joshi wrote, 'In 1967 the concept of coalition government was gaining ground. Wherever we went, people said that we should work in the direction of forming a coalition government in Madhya Pradesh as that was the opinion we gathered at most places. Senior party workers decided that this issue should be considered seriously. When we asked for Panditji's advice, he promised to discuss it in Bhopal. Panditji came to Bhopal and a meeting was called in which senior state level party workers and the MLAs were invited. Right in the beginning of the meeting, Panditji asked for the opinion of each and every participant on the issue. Some favoured a coalition government while others presented their forceful arguments against the idea. In the end, Panditji evaluated every aspect of the issue and said that the stability of all such coalition governments which were formed, or will be formed in future, would be doubted by all. Such coalition governments, he opined, would not last more than two years. He said if an occasion

---

[137]Ibid, p. 24.

arose, it would provide the party with an opportunity to run a government. Keeping that in mind, he wanted everyone to be a part of it.'[138]

Ashwini Kumar recounted how he approved the initiative to form a coalition government in Bihar. He wrote, 'Like his personal life, he also always upheld the principle of democracy in the party. After the Bihar Assembly elections in 1967, an effort was being made to form a government other than that of Congress. It was the general opinion that if socialists, Jana Sangh and communists joined hands, the government could be formed. I apprised Pt Deendayal Upadhyaya of this situation and sought his guidance. Instead of giving his opinion he called me to Delhi the very next day, as he was also reaching there. At Delhi, Deendayalji called a meeting of the Parliamentary Board. The meeting of the Parliamentary Board was attended by Shri Balraj Madhok, Shri Jagannath Rao Joshi, Shri Nanaji Deshmukh, Shri Atal Bihari Vajpayee, Shri Yagya Dutt Sharma and Shri Sunder Singh Bhandari. In the meeting I was grilled for three-and-a-half hours and then it was decided to send Nanaji and me to Patna to verify if what I had said was true. After Nanaji ascertained the situation himself and sent a report to the party, only then was a decision taken.'[139]

A situation arose in Punjab when the state was divided and the question of language came to fore. As Jana Sangh was committed to Hindi language, accepting Punjabi as language for Punjab state was not going down well with many in the party. Krishna Kumar Goel recalled the incident thus, 'I recall the session called after the division of Punjab into two states. Meeting of the national executive was in progress. I was also present in my capacity as the State President. A suggestion was made to the Working Committee to accept the Punjabi language after agreeing to the division of Punjab.

---

[138]Ibid pp. 119–120.
[139]Ibid, pp. 107–108.

There was a hot discussion for hours together on this resolution. The delegates from Punjab vehemently opposed it and many were overwhelmed with sentiments. It looked as if the resolution would get rejected, but everybody was surprised when in the end Panditji asked the meeting to accept the reality. He said that Punjabi is an Indian language and we should accept Punjab and Haryana as two different states and the organisational set up of Jana Sangh in these two states should also be separate. He presented his views before the working committee. The tense atmosphere calmed down immediately. After sometime the working committee put its seal of approval.'[140]

He invoked the principle of wide consultation with karyakartas while ensuring their participation in decision making process at various levels. He believed in the democratic functioning of the party and inculcated its spirit in the functioning of the organization. He encouraged the karyakartas to voice their opinions and listened to them patiently, and sometimes even acted against his own personal beliefs. One such example was when he gave his opinion that fish should be recognized as supplementary food, and that the government should work towards increasing the production of fish, even though he himself was a vegetarian. He was also not very keen to invoke prohibition because he thought that the consequences of prohibition may far exceed the benefits. He was a true practitioner of internal democracy and never hesitated in revising his views after a thorough process of consultation and discussion.

UNCOMPROMISING AND FIRM

Deendayal's concern for karyakartas never overwhelmed his concern for organizational principles and discipline. He was soft at heart,

---

[140]Ibid, pp. 166–167.

cared for the karyakartas, but was also a hard taskmaster and strict disciplinarian. He was uncompromising in principles and upheld the ideals of the organization at whatever cost it demanded. He was firm in executing decisions and never allowed the policies and principles of the organization to be compromised. An instance of his uncompromising and firm stand was seen during the expulsion of MLAs in Rajasthan. It was a very difficult decision for any party, but Deendayal took no time in upholding the party principle, even at the cost of losing five MLAs out of its strength of eight in Rajasthan assembly. Jana Sangh, right from the beginning, demanded the abolition of zamindari and opposed the policy of Congress that provided compensation to the big landlords and rehabilitation and relief to the small landlords. Deendayal was committed to protect the interests of the poor, helpless tillers of the land and the common man. He inspired the Jana Sangh to chant the slogan of 'Land to the tiller'. In 1952, Jana Sangh had won eight seats in Rajasthan assembly, but a situation was created where the party, at its nascent stage, had to take a principled stand and expel five of its members. It was a test for the newly-formed party in which it came out with flying colours. While recounting the incident V.N. Deodhar wrote:

> Seventy-seven MLAs from Rajasthan, out of a total strength of one hundred sixty, formed Samyukta Vidhayak Dal (United Legislative Party). It included eight belonging to Jana Sangh. On the basis of this strength, Lal Singh of Jana Sangh was elected as the Deputy Speaker of the Assembly.
>
> The 'Samvid' planned to oppose the Land-reforms, because most of its members belonged to the Zamindar-Jagirdar section. This note of the 'Samvid' foreboded that the image of the Jana Sangh, too, would be that of Zamindar-Jagirdar group. This was a question of principle and the image of Jana Sangh. What would be Panditji's decision? He directed that the members of the 'progressive Jana Sangh should

resign from the membership of the Reactionary Samvid.' His mandate was followed by three MLAs, whereas the remaining five, including the Deputy Speaker Lal Singh, refused to be led by this order. Panditji unhesitatingly cancelled the primary membership (of the Jana Sangh) of the five members. Panditji had the responsibility to maintain the clean mass-oriented image of Jana Sangh. For this, such an exemplary step for strict discipline was needed.

This means that along with his gentle persuasions, whenever needed, he had the unflinching capacity to enforce party-discipline. He was a magician who interwove the organisational web of the All India Party and used his mass-appeal, power of expression and mostly exemplary behaviour. We have tried to depict his invisible but immortal memory with the kaleidoscopic colours of many admirers' experiences. This is an attempt in the faith that the study of a great man may inspire us too.[141]

Another incident was related to Lala Harichand in Delhi. Prof. Vijay Kumar Malhotra narrated the incident in which Deendayal enforced the principle of selfless service in the organization. He wrote:

During 1959–1960, Corporation Committees were to be elected and among all the committees the Standing Committee held an important position. It was decided that it should either be constituted by consensus or through elections contested in alliance with the independents. Lala Harichand wanted to contest elections for the Standing Committee. In a fit of anger Lalaji declared that if he was not allowed to contest the elections he would quit the party. We did not know how to react on this issue. It was not easy to talk to the

---

[141]Deodhar, V.N., *Pandit Deendayal Upadhyaya: Ideology and Perception*, Part VII, Suruchi Prakashan, New Delhi, 2014, pp. 41–42.

senior most member, Sanghachalak and celebrities in Delhi like him about it. When Deendayalji came to know about it he immediately wrote a letter to the Leader of the party, Shri Kidar Nath Sahani saying: 'I have come to know that Lala Harichand has said that if he was not given a chance to contest elections for Head of the Standing Committee, he would quit the party. It is very unfortunate and I didn't expect this from him. Therefore, it is important to find out a solution to this problem of indiscipline. I wish that you meet him personally and find out the truth. If Lalaji has only one priority of getting into the Standing Committee, then we should reconsider our decision. We never evaluated him so low. How long would we be able to keep such people into our fold by paying such a price? If Lalaji gives more weight to his threat of resignation then Shri Sahadev should be asked to contest elections.'

I carried this letter to Lala Harichand. He read the letter and his eyes were moist. He wrote back, 'I am very sorry for my words which made you sad. I would like to make it clear that I never wanted to create this unpleasant situation.'[142]

He also never encouraged unprincipled politics for the sake of power. In the game of power politics, he was not a participant rushing after power by compromising with principles. Sunder Singh Bhandar recounted one such incident:

Jana Sangh was victorious in 27 out of 80 constituencies in Delhi Corporation elections and the Congress could not get a majority. A wealthy independent member of the Corporation came and suggested that Jana Sangh should make efforts to rope in a few independent members to their side in order to

---

[142]Jha, Prabhat, *The Ajaatshatru Deendayalji*, Dr. Mookerjee Smruti Nyas, New Delhi, 2011, pp. 70–71

get a majority. Panditji showed the least interest in that and had said, 'We do not even have a car to chase the independents. Only those who possessed cars could do that', obviously referring to that gentleman. He left the matter in the hands of the independents to join the Jana Sangh or not.[143]

UPHELD DISTINCT CHARACTER OF JANA SANGH

Many a time Jana Sangh's policies and programmes have been confused with those of Hindu Mahasabha, Ram Rajya Parishad and Swatantra Party. It is sometimes done out of ignorance and sometimes deliberately, to attack Jana Sangh-BJP. Deendayal was a visionary who always valued long-term goals over short-term compromises. Moreover, ideological positions remained supreme and there never arose the question of compromising it for the sake of electoral gains. In the early years of Jana Sangh, many proposals were floated for forming a single party by merging different political groups. Although Deendayal allowed formation of alliances with other political parties, he never favoured the idea of a merger without having sound ideological convergence on various issues of concern. Once there was a proposal for merger of Jana Sangh with Ram Rajya Parishad, which Deendayal rejected on the ground of huge ideological differences.

J.P. Mathur who, along with Deendayal, had gone to meet Karpatriji, a renowned saint and leader of Ram Rajya Parishad, narrated a very interesting encounter between the two leaders. He wrote:

> Deendayalji was a soft-spoken person with firm convictions. In 1953, after the passing away of Dr Syama Prasad Mookerjee, the founder of the Bharatiya Jana Sangh, at Srinagar on

---

[143]Ibid, p. 49.

June 23, 1953, Swami Karpatriji of Ram Rajya Parishad had invited Deendayalji for discussing the role of political parties professing Hindu nationalism. Since the Ram Rajya Parishad led by Karpatriji had earned for itself an important place in Indian politics those days, he suggested to Deendayalji that the Jana Sangh, the Hindu Mahasabha and the Ram Rajya Parishad should merge into a single party. Deendayalji and myself called on the Swamiji, then living in a small cottage on the bank of the Yamuna. Deendayalji prostrated before the Swamiji in all humility. Karpatriji made two proposals. First, let the Jana Sangh be run on the basis of principles enunciated by religious texts. Deendayalji humbly turned down this suggestion. A political party, he had told Karpatriji, could not be run on the basis of any religious text. The second proposal was more outrageous. Karpatriji said that the Dalits, then known as Harijans, should not be given equal status with other Hindus. Deendayalji's response was, 'We do not accept any move to divide the Hindu society along caste lines.' We left after prostrating once again before the Swamiji.[144]

The role of religion in politics was also stated in clear terms by Deendayal many times. J.P. Mathur recounted one more incident where the ideological difference between Jana Sangh and Ram Rajya Parishad was clearly stated by Deendayal. J.P. Mathur wrote, 'It was probably in 1954 that we called on Pandit Nandlal Sharma, MP and the then general secretary of the Ram Rajya Parishad. While accepting the necessity of religious thought in individual and group life, Deendayalji had argued against basing politics or state on religion. He contended that like life, science too changed and everybody had a right to modify his views on religion, and that it was for the state to ensure that freedom in this respect was guaranteed to all. Thus he was the architect of the party's policy

---

[144]Ibid, p. 27.

of respecting tradition but remaining aloof from communalism.'[145]

Deendayal believed that Jana Sangh should have its ideological foundation rooted in Indian reality and avoid following Western ideas blindly. He was not in favour of piecemeal approach to the nation's problems, and emphasized on an integral approach in the Indian context. He had firm faith in the abilities of the common man and felt that India's future lay in the hands of the poor, helpless, downtrodden and deprived. He believed that neither capitalism nor Marxism can solve India's problems, but ideas rooted in Indian tradition, culture, history and its genius can lead India towards a bright future. Such thinking made Jana Sangh to distance itself ideologically from Socialist Party on the one hand, and Swatantra Party, which denounced socialism, on the other. How Deendayal ideologically took positions in contemporary political scenario in distancing Jana Sangh from such parties, yet making Jana Sangh more realistic and pragmatic was narrated by J.P. Mathur. He wrote, 'In October 1956 the party's All India Working Committee was in session at Poona. The 1957 elections were round the corner. Deendayalji was briefing newsmen in the evening. At the very outset he opposed the misleading slogan of socialism. Newsmen could scarcely believe their ears. Correspondents of the Press Trust of India and *The Times of India* repeatedly asked him if he was making a policy statement. The query drew an emphatic "Yes" from him. Many of his colleagues then felt that it was improper to oppose a popular trend at the time of elections. His rejoinder was, it was at election time that one should clearly state one's views.'[146]

Three years later, in 1959, the Swatantra Party was founded and its leaders, including Rajaji, denounced socialism. But there the similarity ended, for the Jana Sangh accepted the concept of social justice implicit in socialism, and opposed only the concentration of

---

[145]Raje, Sudhakar (Ed.), *Pt. Deendayal Upadhyaya: A Profile*, Deendayal Research Institute, New Delhi, 1992, p. 59.
[146]Ibid, pp. 60–61.

economic power in the hands of the state or private individuals. It was not only in this regard that Bharatiya Jana Sangh differed from Swatantra Party, but also on the issue of Kashmir. Swatantra party was in favour of holding talks with Pakistan on the issue of Kashmir, while Jana Sangh opposed it vehemently. Minoo Masani, the general secretary of Swatantra Party, did not just stop there, but also wanted the United Nations to act as a mediator on the issue. A section of Jana Sangh was pressing for merger with Swatantra Party. As a result, an electoral alliance was reached by both the parties. However, Minoo Masani, in a statement, expressed his dissatisfaction on Jana Sangh's stand on Kashmir, following which Deendayal broke the alliance with Swatantra Party and declared:

> I thank Masani that he expressed his views on this issue in such clear terms. His declaration freed us from the electoral agreement which was becoming a problem due to the stand that Swatantra Party's leaders were taking on the issue of Kashmir and Pakistan. It is natural that Jana Sangh does not come to agreement with any such group or party which wants to hand over a part of the country to an aggressor and invader. We do not need the lectures of Masani on what is good and what is bad. The issue of national unity and indivisibility are central to our existence. We will not leave any stone unturned in achieving this goal.[147]

It was during the 1963 by-election when Dr Lohia came closer to Jana Sangh. He could see the selfless karyakartas of Jana Sangh working with dedication. When the results were declared, Dr Lohia had no reservations in giving credit to Jana Sangh in securing victory on Farrukhabad seat. Dr Lohia, while on a visit to a UP Jana Sangh workers' camp, had admitted that in economic matters the

---

[147]Sharma, Mahesh Chandra, *Pandit Deendayal Upadhyaya*, Publication Division, Ministry of Information & Broadcasting, Government of India, New Delhi, 2004, p. 43.

party was more '"socialist" than the Socialist Party itself.'[148] Dr Lohia and Deendayal were known as the architects of 'Samvid' governments after Congress lost power in various states. While Dr Lohia considered anti-congressism as the main plank, Deendayal considered that shortcut to power was not sustainable and Congress should be defeated on the basis of programmes and policies.

Madhu Limaye wrote about Dr Lohia's approach, 'For Lohia, the "distinction" among parties related neither to their leftism or rightism nor to their adherence to Democracy Totalitarianism. It was between those in the government and those who were "out of it". A state of permanent opposition or prospect of being kept out of power produced frustration or a sense of despair. Lohia wanted the Opposition parties to overcome this by joining hands in the achievement of the urgent goal of throwing the Congress out of power.'[149]

Lohia and Deendayal had long discussions on various issues on which they could work together and even issued a joint statement demanding formation of Indo-Pak Confederation on 12 April 1964, where they expressed deep concern over the persecution of minorities in Pakistan. The declaration said, 'Large-scale riots in East Pakistan have compelled some over two lakh Hindus and other minorities to come over to India. Indians naturally feel incensed by the happenings in East Bengal. To bring the situation under control and to prescribe the right remedy for the situation, it is essential that the malady be properly diagnosed. And even in this state of mental agony, the basic values of our national life must never be forgotten.'[150]

The declaration also emphasized that the responsibilities

---

[148]Raje, Sudhakar, (Ed.), *Pt. Deendayal Upadhyaya: A Profile*, Deendayal Research Institute, New Delhi, 1992, p. 61.
[149]Mathur, J.P., *History of Bharatiya Jana Sangh*, Bharatiya Janata Party, vol. 6, 2006. p. 277.
[150]Ibid, p. 275.

of minorities in Pakistan rested with the Government of India. It further said, 'It is our firm conviction that guaranteeing the protection of the life and property of Hindus and other minorities in Pakistan is the responsibility of the Government of India. To take a nice legalistic view about the matter that Hindus in Pakistan are Pakistan nationals would be dangerous and can only result in killings and reprisals in the two countries, in greater or lesser measure. When the Government of India fails to fulfil this obligation towards the minorities in Pakistan, the people understandably become indignant. Our appeal to the people is that this indignation should be directed against the Government and should in no case be given vent to against the Indian Muslims. If the latter thing happens, it only provides the Government with a cloak to cover its own inertia and failure, and an opportunity to malign the people and repress them.'[151]

Assuring the security and safety of every Indian Muslim, the declaration considered it the civic and national duty of every Hindu to protect and safeguard every Muslim. The declaration stated, 'So far as the Indian Muslims are concerned, it is our definite view that like all other citizens, their life and property must be protected in all circumstances. No incident and no logic can justify any compromise with truth in this regard. A state, which cannot guarantee the right of living to its citizens, and citizens who cannot assure safety to their neighbours, would belong to the barbaric age. Freedom and security to every citizen irrespective of his faith has indeed been India's sacred tradition. We would like to reassure every Indian Muslim in this regard and would wish this message to reach every Hindu home that it is their civic and national duty to ensure the fulfilment of this assurance.'[152]

Finally calling for the formation of Indo-Pak Confederation,

---

[151]Ibid, pp. 275–276.
[152]Ibid, p. 276.

they said that the Partition was not natural but artificial. The declaration said, 'We hold that the existence of India and Pakistan as two separate entities is an artificial situation. The estrangement of relations between the two Governments is the result of lop-sided attitudes and the tendency to indulge in piecemeal talks. Let the dialogue carried on by the two Governments be candid and not just piecemeal. It is out of such frank talk that solutions of various problems can emerge, goodwill created and a beginning made towards the formation of some sort of Indo-Pak Confederation.'[153]

In 1967, Congress lost elections in many states and a proposal was to form a government by bringing together all the non-Congress political parties together. Dr M.M. Joshi wrote, 'The Congress party lost majority of its seats to different Opposition parties. It triggered off many rounds of deliberations as Opposition parties wanted to form the government in the states at any cost. Bharatiya Jana Sangh was an important player as it had sizeable numbers in the assemblies. Deendayalji gave a cold response to the idea of forming a Samyukta Vidhayak Dal (SVD) Government. In his opinion shortcut to power would bring no glory to the party and ideology. In Uttar Pradesh he rejected the offer. But in Bihar he agreed. Ultimately, he gave the green signal to SVD Government in UP as well.'[154]

Deendayal was also not in favour of the manner in which political parties were sought to be labelled in India. He felt that importing Western categories to classify parties in India may lead to problematic assumptions, far from the reality. While highlighting the hollowness on the practice of identifying parties along left-right dichotomy in India, he wrote in the *Organiser* on 18 December 1961, 'The Congress may be termed a leftist party in so far as it stands for a socialist pattern of economy, but the support it extends to

---

[153]Ibid.
[154]Jha, Prabhat (Ed.), *The Ajaatshatru Deendayalji*, Dr. Mookerjee Smruti Nyas, New Delhi, 2011, pp 13–14.

and derives from the vested interests lends it a conservative colour. The Jana Sangh may be called rightist because it does not believe in doctrinaire socialism but its programme and cadre definitely make it more radical than some of the so-called radical parties of the country.'[155]

He further felt that even if left-right classification was discarded, one would still find political parties taking inspiration from the West to mould Indian politics on Western model. The Congress, the communists, the PSP, the socialists and the Swatantra who believed that India's future lay in Western idealism, sought to transplant their ideas blindly. He further wrote, 'Whatever differences there are among these parties, they all seek to project foreign politics into the Indian scene. They refuse to think originally or take into consideration the basic thought-values of our nation. The utmost that some of these parties concede is an integration of Western ideals and Bharatiya culture. They want a Western political picture in the Indian background. In analysing the political situation in India, they readily and unquestioningly accept results of foreign analysts. The communists stand for unadulterated Marxism as developed in Russia.'[156]

He believed that while parties like Congress, PSP and socialists remained divided between democracy and socialism, Swatantra Party, which opposed socialism, failed to find any better alternative than discredited capitalism. These parties kept oscillating between their loyalties to democracy and socialism. While talking about Jana Sangh and Ram Rajya Parishad he said, 'On the other hand there are parties which derive their inspiration from the eternal values of Bharatiya culture and life, and are not prepared blindly to accept Western ways and ideals. The Jana Sangh and the Ram Rajya Parishad fall into this category. Of these two, the Ram Rajya

---

[155]Upadhyaya, Deendayal, 'Changers and No-changers', *Organiser*, 18 December 1961.
[156]Ibid.

Parishad represents the more orthodox type and is opposed to all sorts of social and economic reforms. The Jana Sangh follows the reformist tradition of Dayanand and Tilak, not only in the social field but also attempts to extend it to economic issues.'[157] Deendayal not only distinguished Jana Sangh from other political parties, he was also very clear about which path the nation should tread in its quest for a better future. He had the sense of balance, the acumen to gel the present with the past and a vision for the future. He ensured that Jana Sangh was not awed by the achievements of the West or get trapped in the orthodoxies and rigidities of India's past. As a party of the future, Jana Sangh had to remain rooted in India's past, have a realistic assessment of the present and a dream for the future.

ELECTORAL POLITICS

Deendayal considered elections very important as it provided an opportunity to present the principles and programmes of the party and to campaign for them. It also gave an opportunity to the new party to train its activists, while facilitating presence of the party among the masses. While addressing a session of Maharashtra Jana Sangh in Nasik he said that it would be advisable to contest maximum number of seats because in an election, seats and votes both have their importance. Even if the election was lost, the number of votes polled in their favour would be useful in the context of the future programmes of action. It was therefore not proper to think of leaving any seat uncontested. He also said that they would spread the network of their activities in every part of their constituency or region.

Sumati Tai Suklikar, one of the most senior women leaders who pioneered the work of involving women with the Jana Sangh,

---

[157]Ibid.

narrated an incident which reflects how clear Deendayal was about the role of elections. She said, '...one day Deendayalji came to Nagpur. He told me, "Tai, you have to contest election for the Legislative Assembly from West Nagpur." I asked him, "How could I win the election in an area dominated by Congress?" In one breath Deendayalji said, "Tai, when we fight the election, one will win and the other will lose. Who will win and who will lose will be decided later on." Otherwise, he asked, how will the work of the party expand? We fought the election and lost, but the party went on moving ahead.'[158]

V.N. Deodhar in his book referred to Sumanbhai Parikh's story which confirmed Panditji's attitude towards elections: 'Every political party should fight elections.' Panditji would say, 'Just as there is a compulsory question in examination papers and others have options, in the same way, for political parties election is a compulsory question.' But, the reasoning he put forward was even more convincing, 'The masses are in the most receptive mood to grasp the ideologies and compare and contrast them. We should always avail of these opportunities offered by the elections. Moreover, under the programme of election campaigns all the resources of the party are properly pooled. The team of workers can be expanded. Even in the eventuality of a defeat, the party marches forward, the organization gets stronger, more experienced and seasoned.'[159]

While Deendayal always emphasized the importance of elections in democracy, he was not oblivious to the need of upholding democratic values in the electoral process. He believed that elections should be contested by keeping in mind the ideals and principles necessary for strengthening democracy in the country.

---

[158]Jha, Prabhat (Ed.), *The Ajaatshatru Deendayalji*, Dr. Mookerjee Smruti Nyas, New Delhi, 2011, p. 54.
[159]Deodhar, V.N., *Pandit Deendayal Upadhyaya: Ideology and Perception*, Part VII, Suruchi Prakashan, New Delhi, 2014, p. 35.

In his view, from selection of candidate to election campaign to its conclusion, everything was important. In an article published in the *Organiser*, he wrote, 'A suitable candidate to a man of common sense should be one who can represent the party's views in the legislature, who has been nursing his constituency and can claim to air the feelings of its people. As an individual, he should be devoted to the people and as a member of the party he seeks to represent, he should be disciplined and dedicated to its cause. If he has any other qualifications they may add to his stature, but they cannot be substituted for these basic ingredients of suitability.'[160]

He was aware of the manner in which elections were contested. It was on the basis of caste and communal line, and such an attitude was getting acceptable within the parties vying for political space. He was of the opinion that such problems existed due to lack of sound organizations of the political parties. In the same article he wrote, 'Caste and communal considerations also play a great part in the selection of candidates. Congress is the worst sinner in this respect, but other parties also cannot escape the odium. This, also, is due to lack of a sound and solid organisation. ...If other basic qualifications are there, I would not mind to what caste the candidate belonged. He cannot be a casteless human being, at least not in India. But if the situation develops to such an extent that even Dr Ram Manohar Lohia had to forego his candidature only because he did not belong to the caste that numerically predominated in the constituency (this happened in a UP by-election, some time back), it betokens a serious malady. The way out is to strengthen the party organisation, rather than accentuate appeal to caste considerations as the socialist doctor is trying to do by his promise of reserving 60 per cent seats for backward castes and classes.'[161]

He was also concerned with the growing use of money power

---

[160]Upadhyaya, Deendayal, 'Who is a suitable candidate?', *Organiser*, 4 December 1961.
[161]Ibid.

in elections. It was on the basis of money power that selection of candidates and even alliances and merger between parties were done. Such tendency gaining ground may result in turning politics into a business with deals getting struck for power and position in lieu of money. He wrote, 'Financial viability is another big factor that influences the choice of candidates. A number of people are given tickets for no other qualifications than their capacity to spend money. These people come in the field at election time and then hibernate for five years in the crowded bustles of Calcutta and Bombay. They do not come to the people to solicit their votes but to purchase it. For them no price is too high. All that they want is to grease their way to the parliament. For them it is a business deal.'[162] He cited instances when tickets were given by Congress on the promise that the candidate would bear the poll expenditure of the assembly candidates. Such practice had led to Swatantra Party to be commonly known as the party of Dalal Street.

Deendayal was aware of the threats posed by encouragement of such tendency in political process. It may lead to degeneration of democratic culture, affecting the national interests. He wrote, 'All these are factors that are likely to give a wrong direction to the politics of the country. If steps are not taken to mend them, powerful lobbies will emerge in the country's legislatures and political decisions will hardly be taken in an objective manner taking into consideration only the welfare of the people and furtherance of national interests.' He further wrote, 'The parties that want to develop into major parties should be careful not to sacrifice principles for quick gains. People, too, have a duty, and if they exercise their franchise in a judicious and intelligent manner, they can also correct the distorted viewpoint of the political parties.'[163]

---

[162]Ibid.
[163]Ibid.

Deendayal contested elections only once in his lifetime. It was in 1967 that he reluctantly agreed to contest Jaunpur by-election in the face of unanimous desire of the party and upheld the principles which Jana Sangh advocated as ideals, while contesting the election. Bhaurao Deoras wrote: 'During my association with him of over thirty years, I made only one suggestion against his liking and that impressed upon him the need of his contesting election from Jaunpur for the Parliament. The defeat of Shri Vajpayee in 1962 election had created a sort of vacuum in the Lok Sabha. All suggested that Panditji should seek an election to fill the gap, but Panditji was not giving his consent. He contended that being a pracharak, he should abstain from elections as that would establish a wrong precedent and would affect the organization adversely. It was only when all the co-workers unanimously resolved to request Panditji to fight that election that he agreed.'[164]

He lost the election. He accepted the defeat with humility but never allowed himself to compromise the ideals which he advocated throughout his life. The temptation to win the election never swayed him from his principles and, in reality, even in his electoral defeat was his victory. Devendra Swaroop wrote, 'The Congress projected a Kshatriya candidate for the seat. Certain BJS leaders and karyakartas asked Deendayalji to publicly project himself as a Brahmin. Rejecting the idea Deendayalji said, "I am not a candidate of Brahmins but of the BJS."[165] Deendayal himself wrote about this election saying, 'Despite the unfavourable result, my first experience as a candidate in the Jaunpur by-election has been happy. People might not have voted for the Jana Sangh candidate but they appreciated its policies and supported its stand. If the Jana

---

[164]Deodhar, V.N., *Pandit Deendayal Upadhyaya: Ideology and Perception*, Part VII, Suruchi Prakashan, New Delhi, 2014, p. 33.
[165]Jha, Prabhat (Ed.), *The Ajaatshatru Deendayalji*, Dr. Mookerjee Smruti Nyas, New Delhi, 2011, p. 81.

Sangh lost the seat it was not because of any lack of support in the electorate, but simply because it could not prove a match to the underhand practices of the Congress. Anyway, defeat has to be accepted.'[166]

Citing the propaganda unleashed by the Congress, he said that all means were employed to project the Congress candidates, for instance, 'Shri Hargovind Singh, UP Planning Minister, said at one of the worker's meetings that the Chinese invaded India because Raja Saheb Jaunpur, the Jana Sangh leader, had sent an invitation to Chou En-Lai to this affect. In one of his public speeches he said that America would stop all help to India if the Congress was defeated at Jaunpur. Shri Kamlapati Tripathi, UP Finance Minister, in one of his speeches to the press said that the land revenues were increased only at the behest of the Jana Sangh leader in the Assembly.'[167]

Deendayal was unperturbed by the electoral loss as he knew that his mission was not limited to any single election or dependent on its results. He moulded Jana Sangh in such a way that principles and ideals espoused by it were more valuable than electoral victories achieved for some immediate gains. The mantra was to keep moving by having firm faith on the ideals of the organization, to set high standards of public conduct and to educate the masses democratically. Elections for him were an opportunity to educate masses and make them aware of the programmes and policies of the party. A true karmayogi, he was not overwhelmed by victories nor deterred by defeats. Bhaurao Deoras wrote, 'He lost the election. But the very next day, he was present in the Shiksha Varga at Kashi. His behaviour there was very surprising. We could not believe that he was the same Deendayalji who had been defeated in such a strategic election. I also was surprised at the absolutely calm and

---

[166]Upadhyaya, Deendayal, 'Why We Lost—An Analysis', Political Diary, *Organiser*, 3 June 1963.
[167]Ibid.

unaffected bearing of the man who had been in the centre of the fray, just a day before.'[168]

V.N. Deodhar wrote, 'Shri Bhaurao further tells us how the Jaunpur battle had been a contest of ideals alone as far as Deendayalji was concerned.'[169]

Manik Ram Chaudhari wrote, 'On the night of the election result, we had assembled at the residence of the Maharaja of Jaunpur. Panditji was present along with Nanaji Deshmukh. Actually, we had staked out all in this election. So after such all-out efforts, the defeat was all the more petrifying and the disappointment was too apparent all around. Only Panditji was not disappointed. He thanked and congratulated us all for the efforts we had made and added that, "The message of Jana Sangh has reached every home in the constituency through the personal visits of our workers." He viewed the elections as a mode of mass-education through extensive personal contacts and explanations of the policies of the party in detail. This is what we had certainly achieved and Panditji gave it primary importance, whereas the question of victory or defeat was to him only secondary.'[170]

Deendayal's first remark after the Jaunpur election is to be always remembered: 'Our candidate has been defeated but our party is one more step forward towards victory!'[171]

A ROLE MODEL

The newly formed Jana Sangh was not only to be built on sound ideological principles, but a strong organizational foundation was also required if an alternative to Congress politics was to be

---

[168]Deodhar, V.N., *Pandit Deendayal Upadhyaya: Ideology and Perception*, Part VII, Suruchi Prakashan, New Delhi, 2014, pp. 33–34.
[169]Ibid, p 34.
[170]Ibid.
[171]Ibid, p. 35.

presented before the people of India. It required leaders who could gel principles with practice in real life. Deendayal was one of those iconic figures of the party who practised what he preached, and presented a picture of an ideal organizer, ideologue and a leader. He epitomized the idea of selfless service in politics and went to the extent of committing himself for life in making politics a noble tool for national regeneration and uplift of the poorest of the poor in the society. As an ideal organizer, he was not only easily accessible, his simplicity and sensitive approach towards karyakartas helped him in nurturing personal bonds with them which was to become the foundation of the organization.

Deendayal made a deep impact on the work culture of the organization. An organization which groomed fearless and disciplined karyakartas was cemented by mutual respect, love and affection on the notion of collectivism and team spirit. Deendayal himself presented an example of selfless service by excluding himself from power politics, thereby strengthening the organizational principle of karyakartas. He had the sense of responsibility, not the desire for post. He cultivated the team spirit by ensuring participation of everyone. He gave everyone adequate opportunity to participate in the affairs of the organization. He ensured internal democracy in the party and followed the dictum that opinions may differ within the organization, but the decision should always be a collective one. He maintained live contacts with karyakatas through travels, meetings, writing letters and holding discussion sessions while continuously communicating with social organizations, intellectuals, social workers and media. He was harsh to himself but soft to karyakartas. He encouraged them to participate wholeheartedly in the organizational works. His own example served as a guideline for the party karyakartas, making the organization strong and able to withstand adversity and celebrate success in true team spirit.

Deendayal was able to create an organization on sound

organizational principles which survives till date as Bharatiya Janata Party. He worked meticulously to create a leadership which could present itself as torch bearer of the party that was instantly distinguished from others. The credit for building Jana Sangh by nurturing its work culture and organizational practice undoubtedly goes to him. He led from the front by personifying within himself all the high principles which the party adhered to. In his condolence speech on the murder of Deendayal, RSS Sarsanghchalak Guruji Gowalkar rightly observed, 'Let everyone among us make him the ideal for the kind of all-round perfection he had attained. It is not that I ask everyone to enter politics. In fact Deendayalji was the most reluctant politician, had many times expressed his distress at the kind of work he was being asked to do. He rather preferred his former work as a sanghpracharak. I told him that I could see nobody else who would do the work as well as him. It needed his unshakable faith and complete dedication for a man to remain in this mess and yet be untouched by it.'[172]

---

[172]Raje, Sudhakar (Ed.), *Pt. Deendayal Upadhyaya: A Profile*, Deendayal Research Institute, New Delhi, 1992, p. 45.

DEENDAYAL AND THE RISE OF BJP

In a very short time a party completed the journey from opposition to an alternative, and it was possible because of the foundation laid by Deendayalji. Ideology-based political parties are the wonderful gifts of Deendayalji to the country. This is the identity of Jana Sangh and BJP. Even Dr Lohia recognized the efforts of Pt Deendayal Upadhyaya and this was the reason that in 1967 people got an alternative of Congress. Deendayalji promoted the idea of 'Karyakartanirman', and the karyakartas influenced by him were party-centric and the party was nation-centric. At the root of Deendayalji's ideas were the poor, village, farmers, Dalits and people on the margins of the society. Their welfare is our aim.[173]

—Narendra Modi

As Jana Sangh took shape and emerged into Janata Party, and from Janata Party emerged Bharatiya Janata Party, the history of independent India oscillated between various poles, but finally seemed to settle down in a linear trajectory

---

[173]Narendra Modi's speech on the release of *Sampoorna Vangmaya*, Deendayal Upadhyaya, www.narendramodi.in/hi/prime-minister-narendra-modi-s-text-of-speech-at-inauguration-of-full-volume-of-pt-deendayal-upadhyaya-s-literature-532697

from Congress to BJP. It was a journey marked by ideas and ideologies, agitations and movements, changing the contours of politics from election to election while shaping politics through mandates delivered in different colours. A change is now visible in the leadership of Prime Minister Narendra Modi. BJP has emerged as the most favoured choice of the overwhelming number of people who are voting it repeatedly, both in the Centre and the states. While BJP is set to lead the country to an era of greatness and glory, its opposition continues to be relegated to the background, facing repeated electoral decimation and defeat. It cannot be denied that the emerging dynamics of Indian politics is getting continuously shaped by dedicated BJP karyakartas known for ideological commitments and selfless service to the nation. When Prime Minister Narendra Modi talked about this journey, from opposition to an alternative in politics, the name of Deendayal came to the fore effortlessly. Deendayal has always stood out not only as an ideologue, but an organizer and thinker who transcended partisan politics.

India is a great nation with a glorious past. Its journey of thousands of years has been impeded by several incursions, foreign rulers and colonialism. But the spirit of India survived all the assaults and was able to repulse and fight back the invaders, both militarily and ideologically. Independence from the foreign rule was supposed to strengthen the spirit of India, but Congress leadership failed in recognizing that urge of the Indian people. The repeated refusal to acknowledge the underlying spirit of Indian nationalism, which existed within the continuum since ancient past, has seemed to have brought Congress to an existential crisis. As Congress appears to be adamant against the idea of India as a nation, the mantle to take the nation forward towards its destiny, as expressed by the sages and seers, and propounded by Pt Deendayal Upadhyaya in his philosophy of 'Integral Humanism', now rests on BJP. The economic regeneration and overall development are essential components in the journey towards that destiny. As India will rise from its slumber and take its rightful place on the highest seat of knowledge, the world will be rescued from the clutches of divisive ideas and forces that have been tormenting humanity for a long time. BJP, while committing itself to nationalism, development, good governance and national reconstruction, finds its inspiration from the ideas of Deendayal Upadhyaya.

The rise of BJP may be attributed to a phenomenon, the seeds of which were sown in the form of Jana Sangh. It was not easy to dislodge Congress from the dominant position it held in the decades following Independence, but as Congress deviated from the path it pursued during the freedom struggle, it started losing its credibility in people's eyes. Jana Sangh was formed as a political party with the aim of presenting an alternative in Indian politics. The ideas on which the edifice of alternative politics was built were mainly contributed by Deendayal, who propounded the philosophy of 'Integral Humanism' which still remains the basic philosophy of BJP. Deendayal not only propounded a philosophy rooted in Indian culture, but, as a political thinker, he also engaged himself in a wide range of issues, formulating programmes and policies of the party. He is also credited for inculcating a work culture that believes in the idea of selfless service in politics. This culture created dedicated cadres having unflinching commitment to party ethos and its ideology. While BJP was formed as a new party, the erstwhile Jana Sangh provided a legacy which made it possible for the party to register itself on the national scene within a very short period. In the decades after its formation, BJP has seen a phenomenal rise—from 2 seats in 1984, it rose to 282 seats in 2014 in the Lok Sabha. In three decades, the contours of Indian politics have changed and BJP has become the new hope of the nation.

BACKGROUND

BJP was formed as a new party on 6 April 1980, but its roots lay in Bharatiya Jana Sangh which had merged with Janata Party in 1977.

Bharatiya Jana Sangh started a movement under the leadership of Dr Syama Prasad Mookerjee on the issue of Kashmir and national integration, and opposed grant of any special status to Kashmir. The soft approach of Nehru on Kashmir saw the arrest of Dr Syama Prasad Mookerjee who died in a Kashmir jail under mysterious circumstances. The responsibility to build the newly-born political party came on the able shoulders of Pandit Deendayal Upadhyaya. Bharatiya Jana Sangh played a very effective role during the Indo-China war in 1962, and staunchly opposed the policies of Nehru. For the first time in 1967, the Congress monopoly was breached due to the initiatives taken by Bharatiya Jana Sangh and Pandit Deendayal Upadhyaya. Congress was defeated in assembly elections in various states.

FORMATION OF JANATA PARTY AND MERGER OF JANA SANGH

After the sudden demise of Deendayal, the responsibility to lead the party fell on the shoulders of Atal Bihari Vajpayee. He was elected president of Jana Sangh on 13 February 1968. Later in the 15th All India Conference, held in Bombay from 25–27 April 1969, Atal Bihari Vajpayee was again elected its president and the following slogan was chanted: '*Pradhan Mantri ki agli bari, Atal Bihari, Atal Bihari.*' The 16th All India Conference was held in Patna again under his presidentship from 28–30 December 1969 where the slogan, '*Tin tilange, karte dange*' against the nexus of Congress, Communist and Muslim League came up which echoed in the entire country. 'Swadeshi Plan' was announced and the slogan of 'Bharatiyakaran' was presented. In July 1970, declaration was made for 'Plan for Complete Employment'. In January 1971, general election manifesto was issued in the name of 'Declaration of War Against Poverty'. The defection politics in Samvid government and factionalism and division in the Congress had raised the political temperature of the country. Jana Sangh was part of the non-Congress governments. It witnessed a slide for the first time after its formation. In the Lok Sabha its number came down to 21 from 35 and vote percentage also declined.

The Congress was itself passing through a churning phase and Indira Gandhi's leadership was challenged from within, resulting in factionalism and later, division in the party. It ultimately saw the emergence of Indira Gandhi after the 1971 general elections in which the faction led by her returned to power with a huge mandate. In the years that followed, Indira Gandhi established her authority over the Congress Party, concentrating all the power in her hands. The arrogance of power became perceptible in her actions, and undermining of democratic institutions, price rise and corruption started to become issues in the public domain. The student movement under 'Nav Nirman Andolan' in Gujarat and call of 'Sampoorna Kranti' in Bihar started gaining strength as students and youth lent these movements their support on a massive scale. Loknayak Jayaprakash Narayan became the symbol of the movement and the youth started to gather in huge numbers on his calls in various public meetings. Jana Sangh, under the presidentship of L.K. Advani, who was elected president in December 1972 in the 18th Conference held in Kanpur, was at one with the movement.

As the election of Indira Gandhi was declared invalid and she was barred from contesting elections by the Allahabad High court, Emergency was imposed on the country in the midnight of 25 June 1975, leading to suspension of fundamental rights, press censorship and assault on democratic institutions in the country. All leaders were either jailed under MISA or went underground.

The next year general elections were supposed to take place in 1976, but by amending the Constitution, the tenure of Lok Sabha was extended by one year, and consequently, elections were not held. Widespread movements took place against the imposition of Emergency throughout the country and a large number of people were jailed. The karyakartas of Jana Sangh were in the forefront of this movement. Elections were held in 1977; it was a silent revolution in India. Not only the Congress, but Indira Gandhi and her son Sanjay Gandhi also lost the elections. In these elections, Janata Party emerged victorious and Congress led by Indira Gandhi routed. In the leadership of Jayaprakash Narayan, Bharatiya Jana Sangh, Samajwadi Party, Bharatiya Lok Dal and Congress Organization had come together to form one party. After the elections, on 23 March 1977 the end of Emergency was declared. On 1 May 1977, Jana Sangh merged with Janata Party.

FORMATION OF BJP

Janata Party could not last long. In about two and a half years, internal dissensions started surfacing in the party. Congress also showed no qualms in taking political advantage of the situation. To alienate the members of erstwhile Bharatiya Jana Sangh in Janata, the issue of 'Dual Membership' was mischievously raised. Objections were raised on the links with RSS. It was being said that the members of Janata Party could not take the membership of RSS. On 4 April 1980, the National Executive of Janata Party prohibited its members from taking membership of RSS. The members of erstwhile Jana Sangh opposed the decision and came out of the Janata Party. They formed a new political party in the name of Bharatiya Janata Party on 6 April 1980 in Kotla ground, Delhi, with Shri Atal Bihari Vajpayee as its first president.

IDEOLOGY AND MISSION

Bharatiya Janata Party is continuously striving to build a strong, united, prosperous and self-reliant India. BJP envisions making India a strong and prosperous nation, which is modern, progressive and enlightened in outlook, and which proudly draws inspiration from India's ancient culture and values. It wants to build a nation which will emerge as a great world power, playing an effective role in the comity between nations for the establishment of world peace and a just international order. The party aims at establishing a democratic state which guarantees to citizens, irrespective of caste, colour, creed or sex, political, social and economic justice, equality of opportunity and liberty of faith and expression. The party has declared its true allegiance to the Constitution of India as established by law, and pledges to uphold principles of socialism, secularism and democracy in order to strengthen sovereignty, unity and integrity of the nation.

The BJP has adopted the philosophy of Integral Humanism as propounded by Pt Deendayal Upadhyaya as its core ideology. The party has now been focusing on Antyodaya, good governance, cultural nationalism, development and security. BJP has also committed itself to five basic principles called 'panchanishthayen'. These are: nationalism and national integration; democracy; positive secularism (sarvapanthasambhava); Gandhian socialism (Gandhian approach to socio-economic issues, leading to the establishment of a samrassamaj free from exploitation); and value-based politics.

ACHIEVEMENTS

The BJP became active in the national politics soon after its formation. Once again, the non-Congress political parties shared a common platform while campaigning against corruption and Bofors. As a result, the Congress party led by Rajiv Gandhi was defeated in the 1989 general elections. The National Front government led by V.P. Singh was formed at the Centre which was supported by BJP from outside. In the meanwhile, Ram Janmabhoomi movement was started in the country. The then BJP National President Shri L.K. Advani started a rathayatra from Somnath to Ayodhya. The increasing support to Ram Janmabhoomi movement and the growing popularity of BJP made the government uncomfortable. It decided to stop the rathayatra, forcing BJP to withdraw its support to the government. This led to the fall of the V.P. Singh government and Chandrashekhar became the prime minister of the country with the support of Congress. In the general elections that followed, the public support for BJP went on increasing. In the interregnum, Narsimha Rao government and United Front government, with the support of Congress, were formed, creating new records in corruption, loot and misrule: cash for votes, stock market scam, urea scam, Hawala scam, St. Kitts scam, Lakhu Bhai Pathak cheating case were some of the major examples.

The BJP has been able to expand its support base right from the day of its inception. It not only increased its tally in course of different general elections, it once also became the largest party in the Lok Sabha. BJP won 161 seats in 1996 elections. In 1989 and 1991 it had won 85 seats and 120 seats, respectively. In 1996 it emerged as the single largest party in the Lok Sabha. Shri Atal Bihari Vajpayee became the prime minister in 1996, but due to lack of majority, the government could not last for more than 13 days. In the 1998 general elections, BJP registered victory on 182 seats. The BJP leaders were able to form a broader national alliance in the name of National Democratic Alliance (NDA) which came to power in 1998 under the prime ministership of Shri Atal Bihari Vajpayee. Although the government could not survive, as the coalition ruptured due to unilateral withdrawal of support by AIADMK from the NDA, it came back with a thumping majority in the elections that followed, winning 306 seats in the elections.

The BJP repeated its performance by winning 182 seats again. Once again, the BJP-led NDA government was formed under the prime ministership of Shri Atal Bihari Vajpayee. It created new records in the field of development. Achievements like Pokhran test explosion, successful test of Agni-II and victory in Kargil War raised the position of India in international forum. The building of national highways; reform in public distribution system; new initiatives and novel experiments in the field of education and health; fast-paced development in the area of agriculture, industry and science and technology; exploration of new horizons, like IT and telecommunications; and a regime of stable prices were some of the unparalleled achievements of the NDA government. Several effective measures were initiated to improve relations with Pakistan and Bangladesh, to check terrorism and Naxal violence, and to normalize situation in Jammu & Kashmir and the Northeast. To make the nation prosperous and strong, a number of decisions were taken to ensure national unity and integrity. The BJP-led NDA government initiated a new era of 'development-based politics' under the then Prime Minister Shri Atal Bihari Vajpayee and the then Deputy Prime Minister Shri L.K. Advani. It gave a new form of dynamism in the functioning of the government.

PRESENT SCENARIO

The BJP has been marching ahead with their leaders, giving new impetus to the organizational works. Shri Atal Bihari Vajpayee was elected its first president who, along with leaders like Shri L.K. Advani, Dr Murli Manohar Joshi, Rajmata Vijaya Raje Scindia, Shri Bhairon Singh Shekhawat, Shri Kushabhau Thakre and Shri Sunder Singh Bhandari, took steps towards an arduous journey which still continues to inspire every karyakarta of the party. It symbolizes the spirit of the leaders who were uncompromising on the issues of national interests and showed their political will in the face of every kind of turmoil and temptations. They accepted all the challenges as opportunities and were successful in winning the confidence of the people. Who could have thought when Atal Bihari Vajpayee, on becoming first president of BJP in 1980, said '*Andhera Chatega, Suraj Niklega, Kamal Khilega*', that his prophesy would be realized within a few decades? The confidence of the leadership brimmed from the band of dedicated karyakartas who remained committed to the ideological moorings of the party. BJP, which carries the legacies of erstwhile Jana Sangh, has not only challenged the single party domination of Congress electorally, but also confronted it ideologically, with unflinching commitment to nationalism.

India is moving ahead on a high growth trajectory under the charismatic leadership of Prime Minister Narendra Modi with newfound confidence and hope for the future. According to BJP President Amit Shah, it has been made possible by the hard work, dedication and vision which continue to inspire the leadership and karyakartas to build a great India.

The philosophy of Integral Humanism and the concept of Antyodaya have been the guiding principles of the party. This commitment can be seen in the emergence of the idea of '*Sabka Saath, Sabka Vikas*' and the pro-poor, pro-farmer and pro-rural sector policies of the government. The women and youth-oriented programmes have given a new impetus to the society. Can India progress without emancipating the poor, oppressed and deprived? Can India develop without development of villages where the majority of people live? Can India move forward without empowering the women who form half of the population? Can India have a future without energizing the youth? Can India be India without having faith in its indigenous genius and intellect? Can India contribute to the progress of mankind without becoming a model of development and good governance itself? These are some of the questions being answered by the Modi government through innovative projects and plans which are getting implemented effectively. The hitherto neglected sectors are now showing signs of revival and are being regenerated, as focus of the government remains on them. A huge transformation can be seen in every sector under the impact of decisive initiatives and good governance.

DEENDAYAL AND BJP

Pandit Deendayal Upadhyaya was the general secretary and later, president of Bharatiya Jana Sangh. His ideas and actions left a deep imprint on the style of functioning, organization, programmes, policies and organizational structure of Bharatiya Janata Party. Many activists and leaders, who later became the leaders of BJP, had a great deal of training under him. So, it can be said that the journey from lamp (election symbol of Bharatiya Jana Sangh) to lotus (election symbol of BJP) has been inspired by the fundamental ethos and ideological moorings common to both Jana Sangh and BJP. It is interesting to note how Pt Deendayal Upadhyaya continues to inspire such a large number of activists and leaders in BJP.

Deendayal touched almost all the issues that politics can envisage in India, and even went beyond to conceive ideas by giving an Indian perspective to Western systems, which were getting institutionalized under Indian democracy. His ideas ranged from nationalism, national unity, culture and democracy to economy, Antyodaya and Integral Humanism. It may not be denied that the foundation on which an alternative to Congress was created, was structured on the ideas and thinking of Deendayal who could foresee the turn of events as a denouement of blindly following the Western ideas. It was not that he despised whatever was Western but felt that Indian approach was comprehensive and thus more suited for finding solutions to Indian problems. He also felt that the approaches of cohesion, harmony and unity were ingrained in Indian culture and thoughts.

INTEGRAL HUMANISM

Integral Humanism, as propounded by Pt Deendayal Upadhyaya, is the basic philosophy of BJP. A working team was constituted under Krishna Lal Sharma which recommended that Integral Humanism should again be declared the basic ideology of the party. Consequently, in the National Executive meeting held in October 1985 in Gandhi Nagar, it was included as Article 3 of the BJP constitution. From the days of Bharatiya Jana Sangh to BJP, India has been considered an ancient and eternal nation by the party. It propagated the thought that India's 'cultural nationalism' predated the Western notion of 'nation-state'. Integral Humanism is not about individual versus society, but it is the idea of integration of the society as a harmonious whole. It is not an idea of man versus nature, but of integration between man and nature. In Integral Humanism, complete happiness of an individual is taken into account; harmony and cohesion among body, mind, intellect and soul are seen complementing one another, forming a whole. The idea of '*Sabka Saath, Sabka Vikas*' was the manifestation of the same concept.

Integral Humanism symbolizes the uniqueness of BJP and its faith in the efficacy of the Indian knowledge system. Post-independence, when most of the political parties were in the race of blindly aping the Western ideas of 'isms', it was felt that India could progress on the basis of the ideas rooted in its culture. Integral Humanism gave an alternative vision to the party. The party was able to devise various means to practise and implement the ideas of all-round development through a comprehensive approach.

PANCHANISHTHAYEN

The BJP has committed itself to panchanishthayen or five fundamental principles. Apart from Integral Humanism, these are considered to be the ideological foundation of BJP, thus making it a party based on principles. Perhaps, because of practising these ideals, BJP remains a party that shuns dynasty, caste, community and region-based politics. The idea of 'nation first, party next and self last' is the guiding spirit of the party. The BJP ideology is often succinctly expressed through the chanting of 'Bharat Mata ki Jai'. Deendayal said that Bharat Mata is the basis of our nationalism; once you take out the word Mata (mother) from it, it merely becomes a piece of land. He further said, 'When a group of people lives with a goal, an ideal, a mission, and looks upon a particular piece of land as motherland, it constitutes a nation. If either of the two—an ideal and a motherland—is not there, then there is no nation.'[174] The party considers Bharat as mother of all Indians and all Indians as its children. Being the children of the same mother, all Indians are brothers and sisters. As one chants 'Bharat Mata ki Jai', one declares the emotional bonding of all Indians who are one as a nation.

DEMOCRACY

BJP has expressed its firm faith in democracy. Deendayal believed that democracy as such was not a Western gift to India. The basic concept of state in India is democratic. He wrote:

> Vedic 'sabhas' and 'samitis' (meetings and committees) were constituted on a democratic basis and many medieval states were completely democratic. We always put the king under the watch of various ethical disciplines. Our king did not just love his subjects, he also followed his subjects. There are, of course, the examples of those kings who violated these ethical boundaries and rules. However, the public opposition to such

---

[174]Deendayal Sansar, A Complete Deendayal Reader, http://deendayalupadhyay. org/quotes.html.

kings and the tendency to consider such kings as fallen and evil, show the basic democratic nature of our society.[175]

He also said:

Democracy has been defined as government by debate. The tradition of debate is old in our country. But such a debate can be fruitful only when each party carefully listens to what the other has to say and has the desire to accept the truth in it. If instead of trying to understand the other person's point of view, we insist upon our own point of view, such a debate will remain fruitless. When Voltaire said, 'I do not agree with what you say, but I shall defend to death your right to say it', he was only accepting the fruitless part of the debate. Bharatiya culture goes beyond this and looks at debate as a means for the realization of truth. We believe that truth is not one-sided, and that its various facets can be seen, examined and experienced from various angles.[176]

Indian culture does more than this and considers debate as a means of achieving true 'self-realization'.

Deendayal commented freely upon the rise of democracy in the West, its distortion as capitalism and on ideas, like the favouring of dictatorship by Karl Marx. Even while Deendayal basically agreed with the fundamental concept of democracy, he believed that the Western concept of democracy came in opposition to the unbridled kingship and the capitalist-fuelled totalitarian state. He wanted to Indianize this concept. He welcomed the process of Indianization of democracy. The West had invented the process of electing a democracy. It created Constitution, Executive, Legislature and Judiciary. But that was just the formal face of democracy. He believed that the soul of democracy was not in its form, but in

---

[175]ibid, http://deendayalupadhyay.org/democracy.html
[176]ibid, http://deendayalupadhyay.org/demo.html

the ability to truly represent the public desire. He wrote:

> Democracy does not depend on an outer structure. Adult
> franchise and election procedures are important parts of the
> election process, but they alone do not create democracy.
> Both are present in Russia, but the experts of international
> politics are not willing to call it a democracy. Along with
> adult franchise and election, a spirit is also needed to create
> a democracy... Just majority's rule is not democracy... In
> such a structure, there will always be a community, a part
> of society whose voice will be stifled, no matter how right
> it is. This form of democracy cannot fulfil the concept of
> happiness for everyone, welfare for everyone. Hence, in Indian
> concept of democracy, instead of external ideas like election,
> majority and minority-view, the focus is on harmony and
> convergence of different points of view. Even if one person
> has a different view, then we should not only respect him, but
> also try to integrate his point of view into our functioning.
> In England, where today's democratic process has gained
> maximum popularity, the leader of the opposition is paid
> from the government coffers. Just like in sports it is necessary
> to have two parties, in Parliament too, we need to have two
> parties. The opposition keeps giving its view on the policies
> of the government.[177]

BJP's idea of democracy was derived from the saying in the Vedas:
'*Ekam Sat Vipra Bahuda Vadanti*', meaning though the truth is one,
it can be expressed variously. It further believes the mantra '*Vaade
Vaade Jayate Tatva Bodhah*'—the knowledge may be attained through
debate and discussion. Indian society is fundamentally democratic in
nature; it believes that truth is not the monopoly of any individual
or sect. Indians believe that if they are saying the truth then others,

---

[177]Ibid.

too, are. This idea is the basis of the concept of freedom of thoughts and expression and democracy in India. These two sayings, besides representing the democratic spirit of Indian society, have nourished democracy in India. Indians have adopted this democracy in their lives, and in their very nature. BJP believes that democracy as a system is in accordance with Indian ethos.

Deendayal also felt that democracy also meant decentralization of power. If the power is not decentralized, it cannot be necessarily democratic in nature. It is in contravention to the democratic spirit if power is concentrated in any one place or institution. Therefore, in true democratic spirit, decentralized structure should be encouraged. There is a separation of powers between the Centre, the states, the judiciary and the panchayats. There is also a division of labour between them. He wrote, 'The centralization of political, economic and social powers in one individual or institution is a hindrance in the way of democracy. Generally, when power in a certain field gets concentrated in one individual, that individual, directly or indirectly, tries to concentrate in his hands the power in other fields also. It is thus that the dictatorial governments of the Communists and the Khilafat were set up.'[178]

The BJP not only preaches democracy but also practises internal democracy. The BJP is perhaps the only political party in India which holds regular elections every three years, from regional committees to the president of the party. It has led to enriching its leadership from various sections of the society, facilitating individuals from very humble backgrounds to rise to the top rung of the leadership ladder.

It was perhaps the faith in democracy that led Jana Sangh to wage incessant struggles against Emergency imposed by Prime Minister Indira Gandhi on 25 June 1975. As Emergency was imposed, all fundamental rights of the Indian citizens were suspended, even their

---

[178]Ibid, http://deendayalupadhyay.org/demo.html

right to live. All leaders of the Jana Sangh (presently the BJP) were jailed and party offices were locked. The newspapers and other news outlets were censored. It was the most challenging time for Indian democracy. It was mainly because of the deep faith in democracy that the Jana Sangh, along with other non-Congress parties, was able to build a non-violent underground movement, and united the people against imposition of Emergency. Countless workers of the party bore police brutality, jail torture and destruction of their livelihoods. As a result of their struggle, the real power of people was displayed in 1977 and Indira Gandhi government humbled in the elections.

POSITIVE SECULARISM AND 'SARVA DHARMA SAMBHAV'

The manner in which the term 'secularism' has been sought to be interpreted by various political parties has resulted in further confusion over its real meaning. It may be noted that 'secularism' is practised in different ways in the West, and different countries have adopted different versions of secularism. In India as well, it is variously interpreted, and has been given the meaning that suits those with vested interests. Its distorted version has given way to minority appeasement and vote-bank politics. While on the one hand it seeks to patronize selected minorities on religious grounds, its narrative is constructed on the basis of highly biased discourse against the majority community. Hence, it is not only distorted and misrepresented, but creates an ambience for vote-bank politics which is not in consonance with the democratic spirit of our country. Such an approach not only divides the society along religious lines, but also alienates a section of Indian culture and society.

In the first session of Jana Sangh held in Kanpur, a resolution in the name of 'cultural regeneration' was presented by Deendayal Upadhyaya. It was a resolution which distinguished Jana Sangh from other political parties. While Congress, socialists and communists believed in the concept of composite culture, 'regional nationality' and nation-state based upon the geographical and political grounds, Jana Sangh believed in cultural nationalism by considering culture the basis of Indian nationalism. While the proponents of composite culture opined that minorities are culturally different and their culture and special rights should be protected and propagated, Hindu Mahasabha, on the other hand, was not ready to accept the Muslims as Indians. That led Dr Syama Prasad Mookerjee to leave Hindu Mahasabha and open the gates of Jana Sangh for every religion. For Muslims and Christians, he used the phrase, 'those parts' and accepted them as part of Indian life and society. Virtually, it had been accepted that the Hindu society is also responsible, in some ways, in alienating the Muslim society. This fault should be remedied now and they should be shown love and affection. Only then the problem of Muslim communalism will be solved. Considering Muslims and Christians separate nationalities and propagating their special rights were considered to be communal and divisive thoughts.

Commenting on the thoughts expressed in the manifestos of every political party, Deendayal once said:

The analysis made by parties like Congress, PSP, Swatantra Party and the communists claim that justice is not done to the minorities. Bharatiya Jana Sangh does not consider the terms majority and minority as valid. It does not accept this division. It considers India as undivided; that it is One Nation. Jana Sangh has full faith that the culture of the entire nation is one. It does not accept the idea of different cultures on the basis of different religions. It believes in one national culture and One Nation. However, due to some historical reasons, a part of our society has been alienated from the national mainstream. It has also become anti-national. The Jana Sangh believes in curing them. It does not at all believe in supporting their separatist mentality... For us, the nation is most important.[179]

The emergence of secularism in the West is generally attributed to opposition to supremacy of church which dominated every aspect of public life in medieval Europe. In medieval Europe, the Pope and the priests of the Christian Church had become too powerful and controlled the State, too, completely in a vice-like grip. As a result, people started opposing the intervention of religion and religious institutions in the state and administration of the European nations. It was argued that religion should confine itself to personal domain while the state should remain secular. A process of rationalization and secularization of society resulted in the concept of secularism.

Unlike West, Indian society never accepted theocratic state and it always believed in 'sarvapanthasambhava' or equal respect to all religion. India has embraced secularism as equal respect to all religions, sects and creed. It is further explained as justice to all and appeasement of none, and decries vote bank politics-based appeasement on the round of religion. It also means that state will not accept any sect or religion as state religion. BJP calls it positive secularism and ensures justice to all but appeasement of none.

NATIONALISM AND NATIONAL INTEGRATION

BJP is known as a nationalist political party. It remains committed to the idea of India as one nation having a link to its glorious past. Its diversity is its strength and its culture is integrationist. It is therefore, not only a geographical entity but a cultural entity too. Explaining it further Deendayal said that geographical unity was not enough for national unity. Inhabitants of a country become

---

[179]Sharma, Mahesh Chandra, *Pandit Deendayal Upadhyaya*, Publication Division, Ministry of Information & Broadcasting, Government of India, New Delhi, 2004, p. 34.

one nation only when they are culturally unified into a single unit. Until Indian society followed one culture, the basic unity of India was maintained despite many political states. However, since the foreign rulers in India gave birth to foreign-oriented ideologies in India in order to increase the number of their own followers, our nationality came under threat. India, which was following the idea of one nation for many centuries, saw the idea of two-nation theory win. The country was divided and it became impossible for Hindus and other minorities to live in Pakistan. On the other hand, considering Muslim culture different from the rest, the same two-nation theory is nurtured and propagated in India by its politicians. This idea is an obstruction in nation-building. For the development of one-nationality of India, it is very important that India nurtures one culture.

He also believed that the foundation of our nationalism is 'Bharat Mata', not just Bharat. If we remove the word 'mother', then Bharat becomes just a piece of land. We come to love this land only when we regard it as our mother. No land can become a nation, a country, until a community comes to love it as its own, just like a child loves his mother. This is patriotism. It does not just mean loving a piece of land. Many animals and birds, too, love their homes. The snake never leaves its burrow; the lion lives in his den; the birds return to their nests daily. However, we cannot say that they are patriots. Human beings also live on land and they also come to love that land. This is not patriotism. Those who love their country as a community, as a whole, and become one with the nation, give birth to patriotism.

Nationalism and national integration are core ideological commitments of BJP. Apart from national unity and territorial integrity, it also believes in the oneness of its people who are emotionally bonded with the culture, tradition and history of the land. Deendayal described nation as 'permanent truth' and said that state is created to fulfil its needs. He said:

> Two reasons have been given for the origin of the state. It is said that the state becomes necessary in two circumstances.

The first is when some distortion enters the people of the nation. The state is established to control the problems that arise in such a situation. For example, one does not see the police when there is no quarrel. But if there is a fight, the police are immediately called. The second need is when some complexity appears in society and it becomes necessary to bring order in corporate life. The state is created so that the powerful, prosperous and resourceful classes of society do not exploit the weak, the helpless and the poor, and everyone should remain within the bounds of justice. It is only these two reasons that give rise to the state. To regulate the distortion that may have entered into society, to establish peace by punishing the wrong-doers and to solve the complexity within a society so that life of every individual becomes just, honourable and easy are the functions of the state. A third function is an important aspect for the fulfilment of these two functions. It is to establish relations with other states. Hence, security from external aggression is also a function of the state.[180]

It is because of nation's supreme position that other institutions are created.

GANDHIAN APPROACH FOR AN EQUAL AND JUST SOCIETY

A Gandhian approach to society engenders a vision of society devoid of any discrimination and exploitation. It is the basis of the establishment of an equal and just society. Deendayal did not consider democracy the only dimension of the political life. He thought that just like 'vote for everyone' is the criterion of political democracy, 'job for everyone' should be the criterion of economic

---

[180]Deendayal Sansar: A Complete Deendayal Reader, *Nation is Permanent* , Our Nationhood, Selected Thoughts, http://deendayalupadhyay.org/nationhood.html

democracy. Explaining the idea of 'job for everyone' and economic democracy he said:

If a vote for everyone is the touch-stone of political democracy, work for everyone is a measure of economic democracy. This right to work does not mean slave labour as in communist countries. Work should not only give a means of livelihood to a person but it should be of the choice of that person. If for doing that work the worker does not get a proper share in the national income, he would, be considered unemployed. From this point of view a minimum wage, a just system of distribution and some sort of social security are necessary.'[181]

Deendayal explained further, that just like 'forced labor' is not something we can accept, similarly an individual not producing products or services up to his capacity will also not work. 'Under-employment' was also a problem. Deendayal considered an economy undemocratic if it harms the freedom of production. A worker who is not the owner of his own produce, sells his freedom. Economic and political independence are mutually dependent on each other. Political democracy cannot run without economic democracy. Someone who is economically independent will be able to cast his vote and opinion with independence.

Deendayal also favoured a decentralized economic system. He felt the need of a decentralized political system and was in support of self-reliant gram panchayats and janpads. He felt that the foundation of an economy should be villages and janpads. The economic policies which might ruin villages and janpads may ultimately ruin India. The extreme development of our cities at the cost of villages will ultimately affect our national unity. Due to the centralization of resources and power, we cannot escape from the cycle of the evils of capitalism and its reactions. In Indian circumstances, a decentralized

---

[181]Deendayal Sansar: A Complete Deendayal Reader, http://deendayalupadhyay.org/economics.html

economy is a must for the establishment of democracy. Hence Deendayal Upadhyaya said:

> ...we need decentralized economy. We will have to create a self-employed sector. The larger this sector is, the farther man will progress, the more humanity will progress and one man will be able to think about another. If we think about the needs and capabilities of every individual and give him work accordingly, then his abilities can be developed. India can give the world such a decentralized economy.[182]

It is hard to bring back those sectors which are now employed with heavy industrialization. Hence the Third World countries should adopt the decentralized economy centered on villages and cottage industries.

Deendayal did not think that cottage industries are not economically viable in nature. He thought that the belief that big industries earn big profit is a myth; real surplus and income come from small-scale and cottage industries. He was in favour of village and poor-centric economy which can take India out of its economic problems. The concept of Antyodaya, which Deendayal adopted in his ideas, belongs to Gandhian lexicography. The basic principle as enunciated by him is that the measurement of economic plans and economic growth cannot be done with those who have risen above on the economic ladder but of those who are at the bottom. He said that unless the last person in the society is not served, a just and equitable society cannot be built.

Deendayal had rightly pointed out that there are dangers of concentrating power into the hands of a person or a group of people. This encourages corruption. Gandhi also demanded people to have faith in right means, not just in right goals. Gandhi did

---

[182]Upadhyaya, Deendayal, *Decentralised Economy*, Panchjanya, 30 March 1959, pp. 08–14.

not give birth to any '-ism', but his views expressed his efforts to attain a fundamental unity of life.

Basing its views on the beliefs of Mahatma Gandhi and Deendayal, the BJP is against economic exploitation and believes that everyone has an equal claim to the resources of the country. The idea is not to believe that only those who earn will eat but that those who can will earn, and those who are born will eat. The society and the state have to care for all. Deendayal believed that along with food, shelter and clothing, education and employment were also man's fundamental and basic needs. It was necessary to bridge the economic gap between the rich and the poor. It is, thus, a fundamental belief of BJP to attain a state where everyone is prosperous and happy, by waging a war against illiteracy, malnourishment and unemployment.

VALUE-BASED POLITICS

BJP firmly believes in 'value-based politics'. Politics is considered a tool to serve the nation and not for self aggrandizement and power. BJP is committed to establish ethical values in society by making public life pure and nation-centric. It is considered a selfless service to the people and a means to make India developed and strong. BJP is committed to restore value in public life and meet the challenges of moral crisis that has, of late, overtaken the politics of the country. There is a need to practise a set of norms which is value-based and may be able to regenerate the ethical principles expected in public life. It was due to adherence to the principles of value-based politics having cultural moorings, that BJP has been able to carve out a distinct image for itself.

The idea of value-based politics may be taken back to Jana Sangh days when Deendayal tried to define politics on some set norms and standards, determining the course of democratic process on the basis of ethical principles. Deendayal believed that majority-minority dichotomy within democracy was not a healthy trend and it might lead to strife within the society; democracy should also not be about majority rule or about the special rights of the minorities, lest it might turn into mobocracy. If the common will of the people was not expressed within the democratic process it might turn into a rule by the crowd which would be chaotic and lead to bitterness in the society. Deendayal, while quoting from an incident in Shakespeare's play, *Julius Caesar*, said, 'The public that was celebrating the murder of Julius Caesar with Brutus a moment ago, was roused to go in Brutus' murder after Antony's speech. It is difficult to keep alive democracy between the two forms of government—mobocracy and autocracy.'[183]

Deendayal felt that while generating public opinion, the political parties should also aim at refining it with the principles of democratic spirit. In democracy it is necessary to develop public opinion through a cultural process which will lead to mature democracy. He felt that public opinion could not be left on the state machinery as propaganda might result in distortion of the opinion in a democracy. While referring to India's tradition, Deendayal said that India solved this problem by taking away the means of moulding public opinion from the state. It is the task of the debating saints to develop public opinion. It is the job of the state to work according to public opinion. The saints, taking care of the spiritual well-being of the people, keep telling them about the ethics of dharma. As they are not at all involved in the proceedings of the world, they can easily arbiter truth. It is with education and culture that society creates and nourishes values. When we bind the public into these values, public opinion will never create problems by breaking its disciplinary banks.

Deendayal never saw democracy as a tool to gain power but as a

---

[183]Sharma, Mahesh Chandra, *Pandit Deendayal Upadhyaya*, Publication Division, Ministry of Information & Broadcasting, Government of India, New Delhi, 2004, p. 69.

medium of people participation. To ensure that democracy was used for this good purpose. He also wrote on issues like good candidate, good party and good voter transcending political spectrum which still remain a guide for value-based politics in the country.

GOOD CANDIDATE

On the issue of who should be considered a good candidate in the elections, Deendayal wrote, 'A suitable candidate to a man of commonsense should be one who can represent the party's views in the legislature, who has been nursing his constituency and can claim to air the feelings of its people. As an individual he should be devoted to the people and as a member of the party he seeks to represent, he should be disciplined and dedicated to its cause. If he has any other qualifications they may add to his stature, but they cannot be substituted for these basic ingredients of suitability.'[184]

He rued that most of the parties focused on winning the elections than providing good leadership to the country. In such circumstances, many a time undeserving candidates are fielded and people are left with no option but to elect them. He said, 'Unfortunately, I have to say that there is no political party in India which fulfils all these criteria, and the only thing which matters to them is that their candidate should win the elections by any means... They try to give ticket to a candidate who is more likely to win the elections than other candidates.'[185]

GOOD PARTY

India has adopted a multi-party system in which political parties have become important players in the democratic process. So it is

---

[184]Upadhyaya, Deendayal, 'Who is a Suitable Candidate?', *Organiser*, 4 December 1961.
[185]Ibid.

the responsibility of the political parties to decide the course of politics and lead by example. Deendayal defined an ideal party as a party which is not just a group of power-hungry politicians, but a dynamic and alive organization, which specializes in things other than winning power. For such a party the goal of taking power will not be an end in itself but it will be a means to implement its principles and programs. In such a party, everyone, from the highest officer to the commonest worker, will have an idealist faith in the goals of the party. We should remember that this dedication is what gives birth to discipline and devotion...if discipline is imposed from above, then it just displays the inner lack of strength in a party.[186]

Deendayal was not unaware of the compulsions under which political parties operated and even granted tickets to anti-social elements and undeserving candidates on various grounds, in contravention to value-based politics. He listed the compulsions as kings, casteism and capitalists.

Kings: The political parties of India have still not been able to spread their roots to the general public... Political parties sweep aside their political programs. They are just interested in making themselves perfect in winning the elections. This is the reason that even in this age, efforts are made to draw old kings, Nawabs and landlords in the fold of political parties... We accept that this old class of society should also become active in the political arena, but the criterion of giving tickets should not be their being from a royal family, but on their inherent capabilities.[187]

Casteism: Considering caste and community before choosing the candidates also affects the selection process... Every person in India

---

[186]Upadhyaya, Deendayal, 'Candidate, Party and Ideology All Count', *Organiser*, 11 December 1961.

[187]Upadhyaya, Deendayal, 'Who is a Suitable Candidate?', *Organiser*, 4 December 1961 and (2)Upadhyaya, Deendayal, 'Candidate, Party and Ideology All Count', *Organiser*, 11 December 1961.

is from one caste or the other. Hence blaming others of casteism and narrow-mindedness unknowingly encourages this trend... If the situation deteriorates to the point where even a personality like Ram Manohar Lohia has to step down from the candidacy in a particular constituency just because he does not belong to the dominant caste of the region, then the situation is serious. The only way to solve this is to make the organization strong instead of appealing to the voters in the name of caste.[188]

Capitalists: The second most important criterion in choosing a candidate is his economic condition; that how much he can spend in the elections. The only reason to give tickets to many candidates is their strong economic conditions. They do not go to political parties and voters to ask for tickets and votes; they come to buy it... Membership of the Parliament is just a way for them to get richer. Congress and all other political parties want money so badly, that in order to increase their strength they are always eager to get the support of these capitalists.[189]

GOOD VOTER

Deendayal believed that voters could change the direction of politics by taking corrective measures. Unless and until voters exercised their franchise in a mature manner, the ills afflicting the political system might not be cured. If people acted in a mature manner and discouraged political parties to take unacceptable course in politics, a pressure might be created to cleanse the politics of many evils. Deendayal expected the voters to bear in mind the following points while voting:

1.   ...one should cast one's vote for one's principle and not

---

[188]Ibid.
[189]Ibid.

for the party; for the party and not for the individual; for the individual and not for money.

2. ...victims of extreme propaganda, some cast their vote just because a candidate is going to win. In this case no matter what is the result of the elections, such a voter will lose.

3. ...the right to vote is the test of your intelligence and wisdom. Hence do not be disillusioned; do not sell it and do not let it go to waste.

4. The right to vote is the sign of the freedom of every citizen. Being a democratic citizen of a free country, you should not exercise it on anyone's instructions; you should use it at the call of your conscience and according to your wisdom.

5. ...the public has to remember this again and again that it is the public which creates the political parties.[190]

The ideological premise of value-based politics to which BJP commits itself may be seen in the ideas of Deendayal. In the absence of certain principles and commitment to larger goals, it may not be denied that politics can be hijacked by power-centric elements having myopic vision for the nation. The nation very often witnesses politicians misusing their position to serve their own selfish ends and promote vested interests. The post-independence era is replete with the stories of corruption and unprincipled nexus operating in the power centres. It poses a threat to our democracy and also erodes confidence of the people in the system. BJP has emerged as a glimmer of hope as it has tried to practise value-based politics as far as possible and earned the tag of a party with difference.

The panchanishthayen or commitment to five principles is a unilateral BJP ethic. It assures the people of its principled position on important issues and guarantees that it will always act in national interest. BJP is also unique as it is neither centered on any particular

---

[190]Ibid.

individual or leader, nor on any family or dynasty, or caste or religion, but on certain principles. It is due to its faith in principles that it is today in a position of giving an alternative, and winning the support of many.

The Bharatiya Janata Party is seen not only as a political party but as a movement. It is part of the wider movement which continues to gain dynamism and pace. It is a party based on ideology and principles. It has its own unique working system which makes the internal democracy of the party lively and cohesive. Unlike other political parties which have split into several parts on different occasions, BJP has been working unitedly with single-minded devotion to the national cause. BJP has not only kept its ideology intact but also its methodology, and both have been developed and nurtured with time. While it has never compromised on its ideology, it has also not allowed its methodology to be compromised. The functioning of the party has been completely guided by its organizational methods and working system. It has conducted membership campaign, internal elections, etc. regularly without fail. It is due to this that BJP is the only political party which has continued to grow after its formation and has been able to register massive support from the people. Unlike most other political parties that have been shrinking with time, BJP believes in the concept of organization and keeps growing by grooming its karyakartas. It believes in encouraging and educating the karyakartas, and this is the reason that people are getting attracted towards BJP. Regular membership campaigns, training programmes, internal elections, regular meetings at various levels and dialogue with karyakartas have enabled the BJP to keep progressing. It now represents the aspirations of the younger generation in particular, and people in general.

THE LEGACY CONTINUES

The coming year, 2015–16, is important to us all—it will be Pandit Deendayal Upadhyaya's centenary year. The Chaireveti mantra was given by him and this led to establishing a system of sacrifice and hard work. We have to think about how to fulfil his dreams, and work and strive to fulfil them. Party and the government should also think about how to celebrate this coming event. Antyodaya, the service of the downtrodden, is what Pandit Deendayal Upadhyaya had stressed. That is why I say that this government is for the poor and deprived.

—Narendra Modi in his speech in the central hall of
Parliament on 20 May 2014, after his election as the
leader of BJP parliamentary party.

Deendayal Upadhyaya continues to inspire Bharatiya Janata Party (BJP), the erstwhile Jana Sangh. The philosophy of Integral Humanism and the concept of Antyodaya have been the guiding principles of the party. It was in acknowledgement of the legacy that Narendra Modi called upon the karyakartas to rededicate themselves to the service of the poor and deprived on the day he was elected leader of the BJP. It was an occasion of nationwide celebration amid the massive victory of 2014 general elections. What was significant in this victory was that after three decades, a single political party got clear cut majority in the Lok Sabha elections. It was a massive mandate for the party as BJP won 282 seats while NDA won 336 seats. A party which was founded at the time when Congress dominated the politics of the country, it was a remarkable achievement in Indian democracy. BJP is credited for not only changing the dynamics of Indian politics, but also for giving ideological direction by presenting an alternative vision to the country. The challenge to the Congress dominance was posed by Jana Sangh, both ideologically and electorally. The BJP successfully carried the legacy of Jana Sangh forward and laid the foundation of an alternative politics in the country.

After winning the Lok Sabha elections in 2014, the BJP formed government at the Centre under the leadership of Prime Minister Shri Narendra Modi. Apart from this, it also formed government in many states. Today it has got the highest number of MPs, SC/ST MPs and MLAs in the country. It has made its mark from panchayat elections to parliamentary elections. In the process, it has entered many new areas and the base of the party has expanded in almost every part of the country. The party has also consolidated its position where it already had stronger presence. Not only this, BJP has become the largest political party in the world, surpassing China's Communist Party's membership.

As BJP has adopted the philosophy of Integral Humanism, the party has now been focusing on Antyodaya, good governance, cultural nationalism, development and national security. BJP has also committed itself to the five basic principles, and all these principles have their foundation in the concept of Integral Humanism in one way or the other. The ideas of Deendayal, who believed in creating an alternative in politics, have largely helped in shaping the ideological positioning of Bharatiya Jana Sangh and BJP. It may appear a miraculous journey for those who have witnessed the initial years of Jana Sangh and those who have written an obituary for BJP when it got only 2 seats in the Lok Sabha elections of 1984.

The BJP has come a long way in its journey from 2 seats to 282 seats in three decades. It has become the only political party to get full majority in Lok Sabha in three decades, after 1984. The BJP has been consolidating its position since then in various states, and scoring electoral victories one after another.

His legacy continues and his ideas take shapes in various ways under various circumstances. Some of his main concepts are discussed here to give an insight into how thinking on those issues germinated in the time of Jana Sangh and remains relevant even today, when BJP-led NDA government is in power at the Centre and also in many states.

NATION FIRST, PARTY NEXT, SELF LAST

The BJP is known for its commitment to the idea of nation first, party next and self last. BJP always keeps national interest above everything and in the time of crisis, believes in rising above the partisan politics and working in unity on the issue of national interests. Many a time, its leaders express their adherence to the policy of 'nation first, party next and self last'. The seed of such a high principle was sown by Deendayal in the very early days of Jana Sangh. It is a well-known fact that the first prime minister of the country, Pt Jawaharlal Nehru, was a staunch opponent of Jana Sangh and RSS. In 1962 when Nehru was attacked and humiliated by Beijing radio and communists in general during Chinese aggression, Deendayal defended Nehru and gave a very emotional statement:

> We must spread out to the villages and generate a feeling of hope and faith in society and subvert attempt of anti-nationalists to project Nehru as another Chiang Kai-shek. We must also determine that this unfortunate episode is not repeated on the soil of India. In order to save Udai Singh, Panna Dai sacrificed her own son. This legacy is our nation's

pride, its indivisibility, and its culture should not be lost sight of; we should be prepared to make any sacrifice for it.[191]

When Nehru visited East European countries, which were still not open to outside world, Deendayal appreciated him saying, '...He (Nehru) carried India's message to Russia and other parts of Eastern Europe where for the last thirty five years, leave alone a foreigner, even a bird could not enter. We should laud Nehru for flying India's flag high there. It is a matter of pride for all of us.'[192]

In 1956, while the country was facing problems in the wake of reorganization of states, Nehru was to leave on a foreign tour. Some people started saying that in Nehru's absence, various problems may be created in the country. At such a moment, Deendayal offered full support of Jana Sangh saying, 'Whatever differences we might have with Pt Nehru and in whichever way we might oppose his policies...I assure my Prime Minister that, while he is away on his foreign tour, the good wishes of Bharatiya Jana Sangh and its unqualified support is with him.'[193]

NEITHER RIGHT NOR LEFT, PRAGMATIC AND REAL

Many times a question is asked whether BJP/Jana Sangh is left or right, and in the writings of its opponents BJP is generally dubbed as 'right'.

Kailashpati Mishra narrated an interesting incident in which Deendayal clarified Jana Sangh's stand on the issue. He wrote:

I had some unforgettable personal experiences travelling with Pandit Deendayalji. It was in 1963. We arrived at Farbesganj

---

[191]Sharma, Mahesh Chandra, *Pandit Deendayal Upadhyaya*, Publication Division, Ministry of Information & Broadcasting, Government of India, New Delhi, 2004, p. 37.
[192]Ibid.
[193]Ibid.

in Bihar in the afternoon. Panditji addressed a meeting in the evening. He had stayed there for one night. Next day, while returning by train, about half a dozen people were sitting in front of Panditji in the compartment. Perhaps one of them had heard Panditji the previous evening. He enquired, 'Are you Pt Deendayal?' When smilingly he said yes, the man shot back saying Jana Sangh had no economic policy. In a very calm, sweet tone Panditji replied, 'A party which has no economic policy cannot sustain itself.' The gentleman then asked, 'Are you rightist or leftist?' Panditji smiled again and in his unique style replied, 'Brother, God has gifted me two eyes. Why do you wish to make me a one-eyed person?' The gentleman then realized he had met a very great thinker. Then Panditji explained, 'Rightists are those who have lost their left eye and leftists, their right one. If you want enunciation of Jana Sangh's economic policy, then I would sum it up in two words: pragmatic and realistic.' This small discussion became his treatise on economic policy, in brief. His words still echo in my mind. The gentlemen sitting opposite became speechless. They got their convincing answers to their questions.[194]

Commenting on the economic policy of Deendayal, D.B. Thengdi wrote, 'Panditji offered to the country a line of economic thinking which was distinctly different from that of his predecessors or contemporaries on the national scene. This created difficulties for the adversaries of Jana Sangh. They could not dub it "rightist" because of the content of the programme, nor could they accept it as "leftist" as it did not profess socialism. Panditji considered this categorization thoroughly irrelevant to Indian conditions. He was guided by realism based on Indian conditions and traditions.'[195]

[194]Jha, Prabhat (Ed.), *The Ajaatshatru Deendayalji*, Dr. Mookerjee Smruti Nyas, New Delhi, 2011, pp. 60–61.
[195]Raje, Sudhakar, *Pandit Deendayal: A Profile*, Deendayal Research Institute, New Delhi, 1992, p. 53.

FOREIGN POLICY IN NATIONAL INTEREST

Deendayal always advocated an idealist and principled position in politics, but as far as foreign policy was concerned, he preferred a pragmatic and realist position. In his own words, 'Bharatiya Jana Sangh believes that a nation's foreign policy aims at achieving the selfish interests of that nation. It should be realistic, keeping in view the ever-changing situation.'[196]

He was not in favour of determining foreign policy on the basis of different power blocs or high sounding ideas of democracy and a free world, opposition to imperialism or colonialism, non-alignment or third world unity as he considered them to be promoting the narrow selfish interest of superpowers. He believed that another country could become a friend on the basis of mutual interests. He believed that the countries which were not with India against Pakistan have no right to claim India's friendship against Israel. Similarly, he said, the question of friendship with Israel would not be decided through the so-called justice to the Jews in West Asia, but on the basis of Israel's alignment with India in the international community.

Although he did not oppose India's policy of non-alignment, he was of the opinion that it was not permanent and the global situation might change. In the wake of Chinese Aggression Deendayal said, 'Regarding the question of staying away from the two power blocs in the world, we must now realize that the situation has changed. The world is no longer divided into these two blocs; many new blocs have come up. Delhi and Beijing are now two such power centres. Beijing has embarked on a policy of expansionism. We require a new power bloc to push back Communist China

---

[196]Sharma, Mahesh Chandra, *Pandit Deendayal Upadhyaya*, Publication Division, Ministry of Information & Broadcasting, Government of India, New Delhi, 2004, p. 52.

and, in this context, we must decide who our real friends are.'[197]

INDIA A NUCLEAR POWER

Unlike his ideas in economic, social and cultural field, Deendayal was of the opinion that army should be modernized on Western lines. He believed that India should not seek war but always be prepared to face one. The policy of militarization of nation and modernization of army was also advocated, and he said that if required, every young person should be given military training. He was never in favour of the policies of ceasefires and pacts, which he thought were appeasement and encouragement to enemies. He believed in decisive war, if it became inevitable, till the ultimate victory was achieved, and for which defense preparedness was a must. He believed that the doctrine of striking power was the best defense policy.

He wanted India to become a nuclear power. He said that the global powers were leading the world not on the basis of their programmes and policies, but because they possessed nuclear weapons. He also believed that the Chinese nuclear bomb had added to its stature, and now countries like the UK were trading with it.

He believed that India, on becoming a nuclear power, should never threaten any country with its atom bomb, but at the same time it should not be a lone worshipper of peace.

'America and Russia have more than the number of atomic and nuclear bombs that are necessary to destroy this world, but they have not come to war so far. Hence the Congress government should start building the atomic bomb and leave international peace to God.'[198]

It should be noted that when Atal Bihari Vajpayee became

---

[197]Ibid.
[198]Ibid, p. 55.

the prime minister in 1998, he made India a nuclear power by conducting Pokhran-II test, defying world powers.

PLANNING AND DECENTRALIZATION

Commenting on the five-year plans, way back in 1958, in his book, *The Two Plans: Promises, Performances and Prospects,* Jana Sangh ideologue Deendayal doubted whether centralized economic planning could be concordant with democracy, and commented on the need to essentialize socialist economy with planning. While scrutinizing the relation between annual budget and plans covering a definite period, he was of the opinion that real solutions to Indian problems might hardly be sought in political and economy ethos developed in the West. He advocated a new process of thought in consonance with the Indian environment. While critiquing the manner in which planning was done, without taking into account the Indian realities, requirements and problems, Deendayal stressed that only a decentralized cottage industry-based rural society could be the backbone of our economy.

Deendayal said, 'Man, the highest creation of God, is losing his own identity. We must re-establish him in his rightful position, bring him the realization of his greatness, reawaken his abilities and encourage him to exert for attaining divine heights of his latest personality. This is possible only through a decentralized economy.'[199] He said that the planners who were banking upon large-scale industries and highly centralized planning and rejecting 'swadeshi' as old fashioned, were not in touch with the Indian reality. He also advocated the inclusion of experts in planning commission, rather than political representatives, and to make it an effective tool in the national reconstruction process.

---

[199]*Deendayal Sansar: A complete Deendayal Reader, Lecture—4th, on April 25 1965,* http://deendayalupadhyay.org/leacture12.html.

ANTYODAYA

Deendayal in his economic policy always emphasized the welfare of the poorest of the poor. The last man in the society was at the centre of his economic ideas. He said that success of economic planning and economic progress will not be measured through those who are in the top of the society's ladder, but through the people in the lowest rung of the society.' Antyodaya means the welfare of the people in the lowest part of the society's ladder. He said that it was our thinking and principle that these uneducated and poor people were our gods and that we have to worship them. He believed it was our social and human dharma.

Inspired by his concept of Antyodaya, NDA government at the Centre, under the leadership of Prime Minister Narendra Modi, along with BJP governments in different states, is continuously moving on the path of Antyodya and dedicated to the welfare of villages, poor, farmers, deprived and oppressed sections of the society, youth and women. By providing social security to the poorest of the poor, the average living standard is being raised. Schemes like MUDRA, Jan Dhan, Ujjwala (free gas connection to poor), Swachhata Mission, toilet construction, Deendayal Grama Jyoti Yojana, affordable houses, cheap medicines and treatment, etc. are being initiated. Agriculture is upgraded through various schemes and technology, and extensive arrangements for irrigation are being made with the aim of doubling the income of the farmers; heavy investments are also being made in the villages through union budgets. BJP government in the country, inspired by Deendayal, remains committed to dedicate the country's resources for the welfare of the needy by checking corruption, black money and the loot of public funds. The path to 'Ek Bharat, Shrestha Bharat' is paved by alleviating poverty in the country.

SABKA SAATH, SABKA VIKAS

'Sabka Saath, Sabka Vikas' is the direct manifestation of the philosophy of Integral Humanism. It takes into account the complete happiness of an individual, along with integration, cohesion and harmony of body, mind, intellect and soul. Bharatiya Jana Sangh, or Bharatiya Janata Party, considers India as an ancient and eternal nation. The thought of India's 'cultural nationalism' is inspired from its glorious past and is more comprehensive than the 'nation-state' concept of the West. Indian culture has a glorious knowledge tradition, and we have to comprehend our future from this. It also recognizes unity in diversity as a unique expression of our cultural life. In this context Deendayal said, 'Unity in diversity and the expression of unity in various forms has remained the thought of Bharatiya culture.'[200]

In recognizing the unity in diversity and plural nature of Indian society, the call of 'Sabka Saath, Sabka Vikas' has been given for the all-round development and happiness of all.

'Sabka Saath, Sabka Vikas' has become a simplified version of all the ideas inscribed in the philosophy of Integral Humanism. Today this concept is applied to foreign relation and to policies formulated for the emancipation of the most suppressed and marginalized sections in the country. It envisages a process of national reconstruction, ensuring participation of everyone. It works for each while discriminating none. Deendayal said that by recognizing the potential of an individual and integrating him with the developmental process, the national goal may be achieved. He wrote, '...an individual has a multitude of aspects, but they are not conflicting; there is co-operation, unity and harmony in them. A system based on the recognition of this mutually complementary nature of the different ideals of mankind, their essential harmony,

---

[200]Deendayal Sansar: A complete Deendayal Reader http://deendayalupadhyay. org/leacture2.html

a system which devises laws, which removes the disharmony and enhances the mutual usefulness and co-operation of the ideals alone can bring peace and happiness to mankind, and can ensure steady development.' It is possible through acting on the principle of 'Sabka Saath, Sabka Vikas'.[201]

LET'S MOVE FORWARD WITH DEDICATION

His legacy continues in the form of his ideas. These ideas have remained relevant even after so many years. Deendayal used to say that the aim of Jana Sangh was not to provide an opposition to the government, but to give an alternative. His ideas were pragmatic, close to Indian reality, rooted in culture and nationalist to the core. He was fired with the zeal of national regeneration and dedicated himself to the national cause. It may be said that BJP has been able to present an alternative to Congress politics in various fields because it was able to carve out a distinct image for itself. Apart from providing an alternative, Jana Sangh / BJP also influenced various dimensions of Indian politics and even set the agenda at various levels. As we see the decline of Congress, socialists, communists and waning of parties like Swatantra, Ram Rajya Parishad and Hindu Mahasabha from the national scene, the rise of Jana Sangh / BJP appears phenomenal. It was made possible by the vision which Deendayal had expressed in words:

> We are fired by the glory of the past but we don't consider it to be the highest point of the national life of India. We are realistic about the present but we are not restrained by it. We have golden dreams for the future in our eyes but we are not sleepy; we are the karmayogis for realizing those dreams. We

---

[201]Deendayal Sansar: A complete Deendayal Reader, *Lecture—3rd, on April 24th 1965*, http://deendayalupadhyay.org/leacture3.html

are the worshippers of the timeless culture of ancient past, ever-changing present and everlasting future...we have faith in our victory, let's move forward with dedication.[202]

---

[202]Ibid.

INDEX

www.ingramcontent.com/pod-product-compliance
Lightning Source LLC
Chambersburg PA
CBHW030916150426

42812CB00045B/57